Basic English for Computing

Revised & Updated

Eric H. Glendinning
John McEwan

D1726326

OXFORD

UNIVERSITY PRESS

OXFORD
UNIVERSITY PRESS

Great Clarendon Street, Oxford OX2 6DP

Oxford University Press is a department of the University of Oxford. It furthers the University's objective of excellence in research, scholarship, and education by publishing worldwide in

Oxford New York

Auckland Bangkok Buenos Aires Cape Town Chennai Dar es Salaam Delhi Hong Kong Istanbul Karachi Kolkata Kuala Lumpur Madrid Melbourne Mexico City Mumbai Nairobi São Paulo Shanghai Taipei Tokyo Toronto

Oxford and Oxford English are registered trade marks of Oxford University Press in the UK and in certain other countries

ISBN 0 19 457470 9

Designed by Holdsworth Associates, Isle of Wight
Typeset by Oxford University Press
Illustrations by Stefan Chabluk

Printed in China

Although every effort has been made to contact copyright holders before publication, this has not been possible in some cases. We apologize for any apparent infringement of copyright and, if notified, the publisher will be pleased to rectify any errors or omissions at the earliest opportunity.

The authors and publisher are grateful to those who have given permission to reproduce the following extracts and adaptations of copyright material:

p7 *Computing Concepts* by T. Duffy and T. Berchelmann, reprinted by permission of Course Technology.

p19 *Second Guardian Education Source Book*, by permission of the *Guardian*.

p22 GSVQ Level 3 in Information Technology, course description from Edinburgh's Telford College Course Information Booklet, by permission of Edinburgh's Telford College.

pp27 & 79 *Computing Studies* by J. Walsh, reproduced by permission of Hodder & Stoughton Ltd.

p37 'Administration: Establishing a comprehensive backup regime' from *Personal Computer* magazine, June 1993 issue. Published by VNU Business Publications, reproduced with their permission.

p59 'Exploring the World Wide Web' from *Computer Success* by Orbis Publishing Ltd., with their permission.

p63 Page from the Hill Street Theatre website, designed by Saladin Rospigliosi, and reproduced with his permission.

p68 'Desktop publishing: fonts and clipart' appeared in *Personal Computer World*, May 1997 issue. Reproduced by permission of VNU Business Publications Limited, publishers of *Personal Computer World*.

pp75 & 76 *Computer Studies* by R. Crawford, published by Addison Wesley Longman. Reprinted by permission of Addison Wesley Longman Ltd.

pp91,95,96,100 & 101 H. L. Capron, *Computers and Information Systems*, (pages 46,47,52,53,350,351). © 1996 The Benjamin Cummings Publishing Company Inc. Reprinted by permission of Addison Wesley Longman.

p96 Reproduced from *The Usborne Computer Dictionary for Beginners* by permission of Usborne Publishing, 83–85 Saffron Hill, London EC1N 8RT. Copyright © 1995 Usborne Publishing Ltd.

p96 'What is a micro-machine?' from *Computer Shopper*, June 1996 issue. Reprinted by permission of Dennis Publishing Limited.

p100 'Computer shopping' from the *Education Guardian*, 8 April 1997. Reprinted by permission of the *Guardian*.

p107 Reproduced from *Usborne Computer Guides: Computers for Beginners* by permission of Usborne Publishing, 83–85 Saffron Hill, London EC1N 8RT. Copyright © 1994, 1997 Usborne Publishing Ltd.

p109 Headlines 'Fears that new virus causes Internet chaos' and 'Police turning cybercop to net villains' taken from *The Scotsman*, and reproduced by their permission.

p109 Headlines 'Cyberspace faces crucial court test' and 'Net bomb blast injures boys' taken from the *Guardian*, and reproduced by their permission.

p109 Headline 'Crime and punishment' taken from *PC Pro* magazine, with their permission.

pp110 & 111 Job descriptions taken from JIIG-CAL Explorer '99, reprinted with the permission of JIIG-CAL Progressions, designers of careers guidance software.

Contents

1 Everyday uses of computers

Tuning-in

Task 1 We use computers in many different places.
Which places can you link these computer documents with?

Task 2 In groups, make a list of other places where you can find computer documents. Try to say what the documents are, and what they are used for.

Listening: Computer uses

Task 3 Match these words (**1–8**) to the correct locations (**a–d**).

1 games	5 flight	**a** a factory
2 machines	6 letters	**b** a supermarket
3 tickets	7 barcode readers	**c** a travel agent
4 wages	8 tills	**d** a home

Task 4 Listen to the recording. Identify which place is described in each extract.

Reading: Computers in everyday life

Task 5   Tick (✔) the computer uses mentioned in the following article.

☐ home	☐ art
☐ hospitals	☐ banking
☐ engineering	☐ libraries
☐ shopping	☐ film-making
☐ television advertising	☐ schools

Computers are part of our everyday lives. They have an effect on almost everything you do. When you buy groceries at a supermarket, a computer is used with laser and barcode technology to scan the price of each item and present a total. Barcoding items (clothes, food, and books) requires a computer to generate the barcode labels and maintain the inventory. Most television advertisements and many films use graphics produced by a computer. In hospitals, bedside terminals connected to the hospital's main computer allow doctors to type in orders for blood tests and to schedule operations. Banks use computers to look after their customers' money. In libraries and bookshops, computers can help you to find the book you want as quickly as possible.

5

10

Language work: Articles

Study these nouns.

   a supermarket   technology   a computer   money

Supermarket and *computer* are countable nouns.
We say *a supermarket* and *supermarkets*.

Technology and *money* are uncountable nouns.
They have no plural and you cannot use them with *a* or *an*.

Study this paragraph.

   Computers have many uses. In shops a computer scans the price of each item. Then the computer calculates the total cost of all the items.

We use a plural noun with no article, or an uncountable noun, when we talk about things in general.

   Computers have many uses.
   Information technology is popular.

We use *a/an* when we mention a countable noun for the first time.

   *In shops **a** computer scans the price of each item.*

When we mention the same noun again, we use *the*.

   ***The** computer calculates the total cost.*

We use *the* with countable and uncountable nouns to refer to specific things.

   ***The** price of each item.*
   ***The** total cost of all the items.*
   ***The** speed of this computer.*

Task 6 Here are some common nouns in computing. With the help of the Glossary on page 120, divide them into countable and uncountable nouns. In the Glossary, and in most dictionaries, nouns are marked *C* for countable and *U* for uncountable.

1 capacity	4 disk	7 monitor	10 speed
2 data	5 drive	8 mouse	
3 device	6 memory	9 software	

Task 7 Fill in the gaps in this paragraph with *a/an* or *the* where necessary.

The Walsh family have ¹_____ computer at home. Their son uses ²_____ computer to help with ³_____ homework and to play ⁴_____ computer games. Their student daughter uses ⁵_____ computer for ⁶_____ projects and for ⁷_____ email. All ⁸_____ family use it to get ⁹_____ information from ¹⁰_____ Internet.

Aids to communication

Here are some phrases to use when you do not understand what someone says to you.

What does X mean?　　　　　　　*Could you say that again, please?*
I'm sorry, I didn't understand that.　*A little more slowly, please.*

Here are some phrases to use when you need help from your teacher.
What's the English for ...?　　　　*How do you say ...?*

Problem-solving

Task 8 Study these screens. Each shows a program used by a different occupation.

1 Who uses each program?　　3 What did they use before computers?
2 What do they use it for?　　4 How do computers make their work easier?

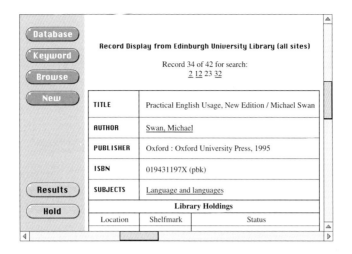

Writing

Task 9 Match the places in column A with the computer uses in column B.

A	B
banks	control machines
factories	calculate the bill
homes	look after patient records and medicines
hospitals	provide entertainment and information
shops	control our money

Task 10 Now fill in the gaps in this paragraph about computer uses.

Computers are now part of our everyday life. In shops, they ^{1}_____.
In factories, they ^{2}_____. In ^{3}_____, they look after
patient records and medicines. When we have a bank account, a computer
^{4}_____. In our homes, computers ^{5}_____.

2 Types of computer

Tuning-in

Task 1   Match these names to the different types of computer.

1 mainframe	3 notebook	5 PC
2 laptop	4 handheld	6 minicomputer

Task 2   Who uses these types of computer? Where do they use them? Make a list.

Listening: Buying a computer 1

Task 3   Listen to Part 1 of this conversation between a shop assistant and a customer. Tick (✔) the correct answers to these questions.

1 The customer wants a computer for:

- [✓] writing
- [✓] Internet
- [ ] graphics
- [ ] video
- [✓] games

2 A multimedia computer provides:

- [✓] sound
- [ ] telephone
- [✓] graphics
- [✓] video
- [✓] animation

Task 4   Listen to Part 2 of the conversation. In column A, tick the hardware items named.

A	B	Device	A	B	Device
		multimedia computer			handheld
✓		multimedia notebook	✓		printer
		subnotebook			monitor
		laptop	✓		modem

Task 5   Listen again to the conversation. In Column B, tick the items the assistant recommends.

Reading: Types of computer

Task 6   Study these details of different types of computer. Find the answers to these questions. Which type of computer is:

1 the most common?
2 small enough for a pocket?
3 the most common portable?
4 used by many people at the same time?
5 used like mainframes?
6 also called a handheld computer?
7 the most powerful?
8 not suitable for a lot of typing?

Types of computer	Notes
Mainframes	Large, powerful, expensive. Multi-user systems – used by many people at the same time. Used for processing very large amounts of data. The most powerful mainframes are called *supercomputers*.
Minicomputers	Used like mainframes. Not as big, powerful, or expensive as mainframes. Less common now because microcomputers have improved.
Microcomputers or Personal computers (PCs)	The most common type of computer. Smaller, cheaper, and less powerful than mainframes and minicomputers.

Types of portable	Notes
Laptop	About the size of a small typewriter. Less common now because smaller and lighter portables are available.
Notebook	About the size of a piece of writing paper. The most common type of portable.
Subnotebook	Not quite as big as notebooks. Can fit into a jacket pocket.
Handheld or Palmtop	Small enough to fit into the palm of one hand. Not easy to type with because of their size. Specialized handheld computers known as PDAs are used as personal organizers.

Language work: Comparison

Study this comparison of three types of computer.

	Mainframes	Minicomputers	Microcomputers
Size	+++	++	+
Power	+++	++	+
Cost	+++	++	+

We compare things using adjectives in two ways.

1 We can compare one type of computer with another.
   *Minicomputers are **bigger than** microcomputers.*
   *Mainframes are **more expensive than** microcomputers.*

   For negative comparisons, we can say:
   *Microcomputers are **not as big as** minicomputers.*
   *Microcomputers are **not as powerful as** mainframes.*

2 We can compare mainframes to all other types of computer.
   *Mainframes are **the biggest** computers.*
   *Mainframes are **the most powerful** computers.*
   *Mainframes are **the most expensive** computers.*

   With short adjectives (*big, small, fast*), we add *-er* and *-est* (*faster, fastest*).
   With longer adjectives (*powerful, expensive*), we use *more/less* and
   the most/the least before the adjective (*more powerful, the most powerful*).

   Remember these two exceptions:
   good – better – the best   bad – worse – the worst

Task 7 Choose the correct adjective. Then fill in the gaps with the correct form of the adjective.

1 *light/heavy* Laptops are ¹_____ than desktop computers, but ²_____ than notebooks.

2 *large/small* The mainframe is the ³_____ type of computer. A minicomputer is ⁴_____ than a microcomputer.

3 *common/good* Personal computers are ⁵_____ than mainframes but mainframes are ⁶_____ than personal computers at processing very large amounts of data.

4 *powerful/expensive* Minicomputers are ⁷_____ than mainframes but they are also ⁸_____ .

5 *fast/cheap* New computers are ⁹_____ and sometimes ¹⁰_____ than older machines.

6 *powerful/expensive* Laptops are often ¹¹_____ than PCs but they are not as ¹²_____ .

Problem-solving

Task 8

In pairs, decide what sort of computer is best for each of these users.

1 John Wilmott is a salesperson and he spends a lot of time visiting customers. He wants a computer to carry with him so he can access data about his customers and record his sales.

2 Pat Nye is a personnel officer. She needs a computer to keep staff records and to keep a diary of appointments. She also needs a computer for writing letters.

3 The University of the North needs a computer to look after its accounts, its network, the records of all students and staff, and to help with scientific research.

4 The James family want a computer for entertainment, writing letters, the Internet, and for calculating tax.

Writing

Task 9

Put the words in brackets into the correct form to make an accurate description of sizes of computers.

There are different types of computer. The (*large*) [1]_____ and (*powerful*) [2]_____ are mainframe computers. Minicomputers are (*small*) [3]_____ than mainframes but are still very powerful. Microcomputers are small enough to sit on a desk. They are the (*common*) [4]_____ type of computer. They are usually (*powerful*) [5]_____ than minicomputers.

Portable computers are (*small*) [6]_____ than desktops. The (*large*) [7]_____ portable is a laptop. (*Small*) [8]_____ portables, about the size of a piece of writing paper, are called notebook computers. Subnotebooks are (*small*) [9]_____ than notebooks. You can hold the (*small*) [10]_____ computers in one hand. They are called handheld computers or palmtop computers.

3 Parts of a computer

Tuning-in

Task 1 Work in pairs. Study this diagram of the inside of a computer. Can you label these components? Compare your answers with other students in your class.

1 hard disk drive	5 processor
2 motherboard	6 speaker
3 memory chips	7 expansion cards
4 power supply	8 floppy drive

Listening: Buying a computer 2

Task 2 Use the Glossary on page 120 to find out what these terms mean.

1 byte	2 GB	3 KB	4 MB	5 MHz

Listen to this conversation about buying a computer and complete the units in the table below.

Component	Capacity/speed measured in	Component	Capacity/speed measured in
processor	MHz	cache memory	kB
RAM	MB	hard disk	GB
video memory	MB		

Reading: The motherboard

Task 4 Study this diagram of a PC motherboard. Match the components to their descriptions. If you need help, use the Glossary on page 120.

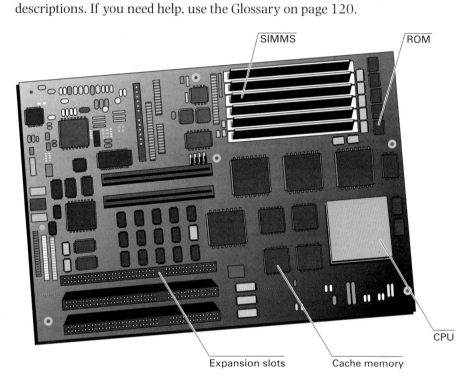

1 These are memory chips. The more you have, the more work you can do at a time. Empty memory slots mean you can add more memory.
2 This is the 'brain' of the computer.
3 It's part of the memory store. It has extremely fast access. It's faster than normal RAM. It can speed up the computer.
4 These let you add features such as sound or a modem to your computer.
5 This kind of memory contains all the instructions your computer needs to activate itself when you switch on. Unlike RAM, its contents are retained when you switch off.

Task 5   Study these instructions for replacing the motherboard in a PC. Match the instructions to each picture. The pictures are in the correct order.

a   Add the processor.
b   Fit the new motherboard.
c   Remove the old motherboard.
d   Put it back together.
e   Add the memory. Don't touch the contacts.

Language work: Making instructions

Note how we make simple instructions in English.

Add the memory.   ***Don't touch*** *the contacts.*

We can show the order of instructions by numbering them (1, 2, 3, etc.) or by using sequence words like these:

First, ...
Then ...
Next, ...
After that, ...
Finally, ...

Task 6   Study these instructions for virus-checking a disk. Fill in the gaps with verbs from this list. Use *Don't* where appropriate.

click	exit	put	select	start

1   _____ the disk into the drive.

2   _____ the virus checking program.

3   _____ the drive to be checked.

4   _____ the 'Find' button.

5   _____ the program until the check is complete.

6   _____ 'Yes' or 'No' for checking another disk.

Task 7 Study these instructions for formatting a disk in Microsoft Windows. Write the instructions in the correct order (**1–6**), using sequence words. You will have to use one of the words more than once.

a 5 Select 'OK' to start formatting the disk.

b 2 Choose 'Format' from the drop-down menu.

c 4 Click the 'Start' button.

d 1 Put the disk into the drive.

e 3 Choose the formatting options you require.

f 6 Click the 'OK' button when formatting is complete.

Problem-solving

Task 8 Work in pairs. Study this diagram. It shows the ports at the back of a desktop PC. With the help of the text below, match these labels to the correct ports.

1 keyboard	3 parallel port	5 serial ports
2 COM1	4 video port	6 USB port

a b   c   d   e   f

Mouse ___ ___ COM 2 ___ ___ VGA

g

___

Desktop PC ports and connectors

External devices connect to ports at the back of the computer. Different types of port are used for each device. Most computers have: 1 keyboard port, 1 video port, 2 serial ports, 1 parallel port. Some also have a mouse port and one or more USB ports.

The mouse port and the keyboard port look exactly the same   5
but they have labels to avoid confusion. If there is no mouse port, a serial mouse can be used. This connects with one of the serial ports. You can use the other one for a modem. The serial ports often have the labels COM1 and COM2.

The monitor connects to the video (VGA) port. The printer uses   10
the larger parallel port. A variety of peripherals can be connected through the USB ports.

Writing

Task 9 Complete this description of the motherboard shown on page 15 by adding the definitions from the Reading text in the correct places.

The most important electronic part of a computer is the motherboard. The largest chip is the processor. The board also contains plug-in chips. One type contains ROM. A number of chips are mounted on memory boards. A third type of memory is cache memory. The board also has expansion slots.

4 Keyboard and mouse

Tuning-in

Task 1 Match these key abbreviations with their full names.

1 Esc		a	Alternate
2 Alt		b	Page Up
3 Ctrl		c	Delete
4 Pgdn		d	Insert
5 Pgup		e	Escape
6 Ins		f	Page Down
7 Del		g	Control

Listening: The keyboard

Task 2 Study this keyboard. The keys are in four sections. Can you name any of the sections?

Task 3 Locate these keys on the keyboard as quickly as you can. Number them 1 to 8.

☐ Insert	☐ minus	☐ plus	☐ Delete
☐ comma	☐ F1	☐ Print Screen	☐ Escape

Task 4 Listen to this description of the keyboard in Task 2. Label each section of the diagram.

18

Reading: The mouse

Task 5 Study this diagram which explains how a common type of mouse works.
Then complete each of these statements with one word.

1 Move the mouse to the left and the cursor moves to the _____ .
2 The mouse contains a rolling _____ .
3 There are _____ axles inside the mouse and two interrupter
   wheels.
4 When you move the mouse, the ball _____ .
5 The mouse moves over a mouse _____ .

Task 6 Now read this text to check your answers.

> The computer mouse is a hand-operated device that lets you control
> more easily the location of the pointer on your screen. You can make
> selections and choices with the mouse button.
>   The mouse contains a rubber-coated ball that rests on the surface
> of your working area or a mousemat. When the mouse is moved   5
> over that surface, the ball rolls.
>   The ball's movements up and down, and left and right, turn the
> two axles inside the mouse. As they turn, detectors register the
> changing position. A small integrated circuit inside the mouse sends
> signals to the operating system, which instructs it to move the   10
> pointer on your screen.

Language work: Present simple

Study these statements about keys.

1   This key *moves* the cursor down.

2   This key *copies* the screen display.

3   This key *doesn't have* a fixed function.

The verbs in italics are in the **Present simple**. We use the **Present simple** to describe things which are always true.

Task 7   Look at the statements (1–7) and correct the ones which are wrong.

Example   This key moves the cursor down.
It doesn't move the cursor down. It moves the cursor up.

If you are not sure, ask another student.
What does this key do?

1   This key moves the cursor down.

2   This key moves the cursor to the right.

3   This key inserts a character.

4   This key copies the screen display.

5   This key moves the screen up.

6   This key doesn't have a fixed function.

7   This key gives you all lower case letters.

Problem-solving

Task 8   Using the information from the **Listening** on page 18, and in Task 7, describe what these keys do.

1   2   3   4

Speaking

Task 9 Match these symbols with their names to complete this table.

| a @ | b / | c ~ | d : | e . | f __ |

Symbol	Name	Symbol	Name
☐	colon	☐	forward slash
☐	tilde	☐	at
☐	underscore	☐	dot, stop

Task 10 Work in pairs. Student A should turn to page 118. Student B should turn to page 119. Read these email and website addresses to your partner. Copy down the addresses your partner reads to you.

1 _____

2 _____

3 _____

4 _____

5 _____

Writing

Task 11 With the help of this table and the **Listening** on page 18, write a brief description of a keyboard. The first paragraph is done for you.

Section	Location	Main keys	Main function
Main keyboard	centre	each letter digits 0–9 punctuation common symbols	input all kinds of data
Function keys	top	F1–F12	not fixed can program them
Editing keys	right	cursor keys insert, delete	control cursor
Numeric keypad	far right	digits 0–9 mathematical operations	input numerical data

Most keyboards have four sections. The main keyboard has keys for each letter and the digits 0 to 9. It also has keys for punctuation and other common symbols. It is used for inputting all kinds of data.

5 Interview: Student

In this unit you will hear an interview with Lynsey, a student of Information Technology at a Scottish college of further education.

Tuning-in

Task 1 Study this description of Lynsey's course. Answer these questions.

1 What is the course called?
2 How long does it last?
3 What do you think these subjects are about?
  Communications   Numeracy

GSVQ Level 3 in Information Technology

Length of course One year full-time starting in August

Course content **You undertake core modules in:**
- Communications
- Computer hardware: operation and maintenance
- Computer software
- Contemporary issues
- Information systems
- Introduction to computer networks
- Information technology in business and industry
- The individual in industry and work
- Introduction to programming
- Information technology
- Numeracy
- Problem-solving

You also select optional units from:
- Accounting
- Programming
- Mathematics
- Systems analysis

Listening

Task 2 Now listen to Part 1 of the interview. Which of the questions in Task 1 does it answer?

Task 3 Listen again to find the answers to these questions.

1 How many students are on the course now?
2 How many female students are there?

Task 4   Here is Lynsey's weekly timetable. Some of the information is missing. Before you listen, try to answer these questions about the timetable.

1 What time does she start each day?
2 When does she finish?
3 Who teaches her Computer Software?
4 Which classroom is Information Systems in?
5 When is her lunch break?

	Period 1 09.00–11.00		Period 2 11.30–13.30		Period 3 14.30–16.30
	Department of Computing and Office Technology				
	Group: GSVQ Level 3				
MON	Communications 4 L. Maxwell 4607	C O F F E E		L U N C H	
TUE			Computer Software Wendy Bright K216		
WED					
THUR	Information Technology 3 Wendy Bright K303	B R E A K	Information Systems Tom Williams K302	B R E A K	
FRI			Computer Programming Helen Hill K201		
	Course Tutor: Fiona Wright, 125 3904, Room K104				

Task 5   Now listen to Part 2 of the interview to complete the blanks in the timetable.

Task 6   Listen again to Part 2 of the interview to find the answers to these questions.

1 What does she have on Mondays at 9.00?
2 What does she study in Programming?
3 What happens in the Software class?
4 What does she do on Wednesdays?
5 What happens in Hardware?
6 What does she study in Networks?
7 What does she do after each visit?

Task 7   Now listen to Part 3 of the interview to find the answers to these questions.

1 Who was at the Students' Night?
2 Where was it?
3 What sport do they play?
4 What does the Students' Union do?
5 What does Lynsey do for two nights a week?
6 Does she want a career in catering?

23

Task 8 Look at the answers 1–10.
Make a question about Lynsey and
her timetable for each answer.

Example   A: She studies Information Technology.
B: *What does she study?*

1 They start at 9.00.
2 She works in a hotel.
3 Ms Murray teaches numeracy.
4 They last for two hours.
5 She goes on visits on Wednesdays.
6 She studies at Telford College.
7 It lasts for one year.
8 She writes a report after each visit.
9 They organize discos.
10 She works two nights a week.

Writing

Task 9 Write your own timetable in English. The subject list in Task 1 may help you.

Days	Times
Monday	_____
Tuesday	_____
Wednesday	_____
Thursday	_____
Friday	_____
Saturday	_____

Computing words and abbreviations

Task 10 Match each word from column A (**1–8**) with its partner from column B (**a–h**) to make a computing term. All of these terms are from the previous units.

A	B
1 memory	a code
2 power	b key
3 function	c drive
4 expansion	d supply
5 bar	e card
6 floppy	f chip
7 disk	g memory
8 cache	h disk

6 Input devices

Tuning-in

Task 1 Match these pictures of input devices with their names.

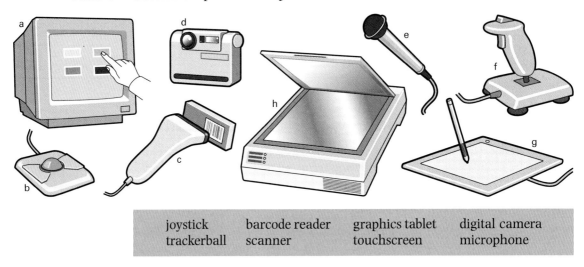

joystick	barcode reader	graphics tablet	digital camera
trackerball	scanner	touchscreen	microphone

Task 2 In pairs, try to list the uses of these devices.

Listening: Voice input

Task 3 Study this diagram. It shows how voice input works. Label the steps in the process with these captions (**a–e**).

Speech recognition board

01100110 = hid
01100111 = head
01101000 = had

a The computer compares the binary code with its stored vocabulary.
b The user says a word into a microphone.
c The screen displays the correct word.
d The speech recognition board converts the signals into binary numbers.
e The microphone converts the word from audio signals into electrical signals.

Task 4 Now listen to the recording to check your answer.

Reading: Input devices

Task 5 Each text describes one of these devices: trackerball, joystick, lightpen, scanner. Identify the device each text describes. Write your answers in this table. Then compare your answers with other students.

Text	Device
1	_____
2	_____
3	_____
4	_____

1   A ____ is another input device you can connect to a computer system. The ____ is able to move in eight directions. ____ s are mostly used in computer games to control the way a picture on the screen moves. Sometimes two ____ s are connected to a computer so two people can play the game at the same time.

2   A ____ works in exactly the same way as a mouse, except that the ball is on top. The user rolls the ball around with her hand to operate it. If you use a ____ , you don't need any extra space on your desk to move it around (like you do with a mouse). ____ s are often used on small portable computers and on some video game machines.

3   A ____ can be used to draw pictures directly on to a computer screen or to read the pattern on a barcode. A ____ that can read barcodes detects the difference between the light reflected from a black barcode line and its lighter background.

4   Using a ____ , you can input printed drawings, photographs, or text directly into a computer. A ____ works like a photocopier – a light is shone on the material and the ____ detects the reflected light. You can use a ____ with optical character recognition (OCR) software to input the scanned text into a word processing package.

Language work: Function

We can describe the function or use of a device in different ways.
Study these examples.

*Joysticks **are used in** computer games.*
*Using a scanner, **you can** input printed drawings directly into a computer.*
***You can use** a scanner **to** input text.*
*A microphone **is used for** inputting sound.*

Task 6   Match each device (**1–7**) with its use (**a–g**).

Device	Use
1 joystick	**a** draw pictures on to a computer screen
2 lightpen	**b** copy documents
3 scanner	**c** input sound
4 digital camera	**d** input text
5 mouse	**e** select from a menu
6 keyboard	**f** move the cursor rapidly
7 microphone	**g** produce photos without film

Task 7   Describe the use of each device in a sentence.
Use these structures from the *Language work* section.

... is/are used in ...
... is/are used for ... -ing
Using ..., you can ...
You can use ... to ...

Example   *You use a mouse to select from a menu.*

Problem-solving

Task 8   In groups, decide which input device is best for:
1   controlling fast-moving objects in a game
2   reading the price of things in a shop
3   making copies of a page of text and graphics
4   storing sounds on a computer
5   producing pictures of people and places for storing in a computer
6   controlling a computer using speech
7   typing text into a computer.

Writing

Task 9 With the help of this diagram, fill in the blanks in this comparison of digital cameras and film cameras.

Digital cameras don't use film. You take pictures on to solid state memory. Then you ¹_____ them to a ²_____ . You can ³_____ and improve the pictures in your PC. Then you can ⁴_____ them, add them to your ⁵_____ , or ⁶_____ them on the screen.

Digital cameras are more ⁷_____ than film cameras but the cost for each picture is lower because there is no ⁸_____ . It's also easy to ⁹_____ the pictures.

Film cameras are cheaper but each picture costs a lot because there are ¹⁰_____ costs. The quality of film camera pictures is much ¹¹_____ than digital cameras but you have to ¹²_____ the pictures to transfer images to a PC.

Digital cameras

Film cameras

7 Output devices

Tuning-in

Task 1 Think about a typical workstation. Match the items (1–7) to the guidelines (**a–g**).

1 keyboard	4 copyholder	7 printer
2 monitor screen	5 chair	
3 lamp	6 footrest	

a This should be adjustable and provide good back support.

b This should be more than a metre away from you and as quiet as possible.

c Keep this level with your eyes. Don't have it level with the desk. Make sure it is flicker-free, and that you can read everything easily. Avoid any glare from the window.

d Use this if your feet do not rest flat on the floor.

e Make sure this lights your work and not the screen.

f Don't get a stiff neck. Use this when you enter a lot of data.

g Keep this directly in front of you and within easy reach.

Listening: Printers

Task 2 Work in groups of three: **A**, **B**, and **C**. You are going to hear about three kinds of printer. Note down what the speaker says about one type only as your teacher directs. Use the table below.

Type	Print quality	Speed	Running costs	Noise level	Price	Colour
Inkjet	lowest	slower than laser				
Mono laser	high			quiet		
Dye sublimation		slow				yes

Task 3 Now exchange information with other students in your group to complete the table for all three kinds of printer. Ask questions like these.

What's the print quality like?

How fast is it?

Does it cost a lot to run?

How noisy is it?

Is it expensive?

Reading: How to read a monitor ad

Task 4   Study this text about monitors. Then decide if each statement is true or false. Give reasons for your answers.

1 Twenty-two inches is a common monitor size.
2 A dot pitch of 0.31mm is better than one of 0.25mm.
3 A maximum resolution of 1600×1200 is better than 1280×1024.
4 A refresh rate of 85Hz is better than one of 75Hz.
5 A 17-inch monitor is 17 inches wide.
6 You can change the picture using controls on the screen.
7 The price of a monitor depends only on the size.
8 The monitor uses less power because of the Power-Saver feature.

£210

- 17-inch (43.2cm) Trinitron monitor
- 0.25mm aperture grill pitch
- Maximum resolution:
  1280 x 1024, 85Hz
- TCO-99, MPR-II, TUV
  Ergonomics approved
- Power-Saver TM
- On-screen menu

AIKIA

Price
The price mainly depends on the screen size. Common monitor sizes are 15-inch, 17-inch, 19-inch, and 21-inch. The price also depends on aperture grill pitch, resolution, and the number of controls.

Screen size
The size of the screen is the diagonal distance from one corner to another. The actual area for images is smaller than this.   5

Aperture grill pitch
This controls the space between the dots which make up the image. The less space between the dots, the better the display.
Most monitors offer 0.25mm dot pitch but some go as high as 0.31mm or as low as 0.22mm.

Maximum resolution
The quality of the display depends on the number of dots which   10
make up the image. The more dots, the better the display.

Refresh rate
The monitor refreshes the image on the screen all the time. The faster this happens, the less the screen flickers. You should have a refresh rate of at least 72Hz.

Safety standards
These are international standards to control harmful signals.   15

Power-saving feature
The power the monitor uses automatically reduces when it is not in use.

On-screen menu
Digital controls on the screen allow you to adjust the image.

Task 5 Work in pairs, **A** and **B**. Each of you has details of a monitor. Ask your partner about his/her monitor and complete the table below.

Student A Your monitor details are on page 118.
Student B Your monitor details are on page 119.

Screen size	_____
Aperture grill pitch	_____
Maximum resolution	_____
Refresh rate	_____
Price	_____

Language work: Giving advice

You can advise people in different ways. Study these examples.

Advising people to do something:
>   *Why don't you buy an inkjet?*
>   *(I think) you should buy a laser.*

Advising people not to do something:
>   *Don't buy a dot-matrix.*
>   *You shouldn't buy a laser.*

To make your advice more effective, add a reason.

advice	reason
Why don't you buy an inkjet?	*They're very quiet.*
(I think) you should buy a laser.	*The print quality is excellent.*
Don't buy a dot-matrix.	*They're very noisy.*
You shouldn't buy a laser.	*They're very expensive.*

We use *too* to make our advice stronger, almost a warning. Study these examples.
>   *You should adjust your monitor. It's **too** bright.*
>   *You should move your printer. It's **too** close.*

Task 6 Advise the user of this workstation on improvements she should make.

Example *I think you should use a chair with back support. It's more comfortable.*

Problem-solving

Task 7 Work in pairs. Study this flowchart for choosing a printer. Decide which is the best kind of printer for these users.

Someone who needs to:

1 print forms with two parts
2 print high quality black and white copies
3 print a lot of colour photos in a short time
4 print a few copies – colour and speed are not important
5 print a few pages in colour.

Writing

Task 8 Fill in the gaps in this comparison of printers.

There are many different types of printer. These include inkjet, mono laser, and dye sublimation printers. Basically, you get what you pay for. The more you pay, the better the printer.

Inkjet printers are the ^{1}_____, but their print ^{2}_____ is not as ^{3}_____ as the other two types of printer. They are ^{4}_____ to run compared to mono laser printers, but are able to print in colour. Inkjets are the ^{5}_____ of the three types of printer.

Mono laser printers are ^{6}_____ expensive than inkjet printers, but give you a ^{7}_____ quality of black and white output. They cannot print in colour, but are the ^{8}_____ type of printer and cost the ^{9}_____ to run.

Dye sublimation printers are the ^{10}_____ expensive type of printer, but their print quality is extremely ^{11}_____. They are ^{12}_____ in operation, but are relatively ^{13}_____ and very ^{14}_____ to run.

8 Storage devices

Tuning-in

Task 1   Study these rules for CD-ROM and floppy disk care. Tick (✔) things to do and cross (✘) things not to do. Then compare your choice with a partner.

1 ☐ Hold a CD-ROM by the edges.
2 ☐ Keep the optical/silver side of a CD-ROM clean.
3 ☐ Smoke when you use your CD-ROM drive.
4 ☐ Put floppy disks near a magnet.
5 ☐ Keep disks away from the sun and excessive heat.
6 ☐ Write the contents on the label on your floppy disk.
7 ☐ Put extra labels on floppy disks.
8 ☐ Remove by force a disk stuck in the drive.
9 ☐ Remove a disk when the drive light is on.

Listening: Hard disk drive

Task 2   Study this diagram of a hard disk drive. Match these labels to the diagram.

1 ☐ drive motor
2 ☐ sealed case
3 ☐ disks
4 ☐ read/write heads
5 ☐ head motor
6 ☐ gap between disks

Task 3   Listen to Part 1 of this description of a hard disk drive to check your answers.

Task 4   Study this diagram. Answer these questions.
1 What sort of things can damage a hard disk?
2 How big is the gap between the read/write heads and the disk?
3 How can we protect a disk drive from damage?

Task 5   Now listen to Part 2 of the description to check your answers.

Reading: Storage devices

Task 6   There are many different kinds of storage device for computers, and developments are taking place all the time. List the storage devices mentioned in this unit so far. List any other storage devices you know.

Task 7   Work in groups of three. Read two texts each and complete your sections of the table.

Medium	Advantages	Disadvantages
Floppy disk	_____	_____
Fixed hard disk	_____	_____
Removable hard disk	_____	_____
CD-ROM disk	_____	_____
Magneto-optical disk	_____	_____
Magnetic tape	_____	_____

A   Most computers use floppy disks. Floppies conform to a standard and you can use them to carry data from one place to another. They are also very cheap, but they are slow and have a limited capacity.

B   Almost all desktop computers have hard disks. They are fast and can store much greater amounts of data than floppies, but they are fixed inside the computer and you cannot use them to transfer data.

C   You can move data from place to place using removable hard disks. They are almost as fast as fixed hard disks and also have high capacities, but they are relatively expensive. They do not all conform to one standard and they are not very common.

D   CD-ROM disks are very common and conform to a standard. They are removable and can hold about 640MB. They are also cheap to make. However, they are usually read-only. You cannot change the information on them. They are also slow compared to hard disks.

E   Magneto-optical disks are like CD-ROMs, but you can write data on to them. They are removable, have large capacities, and last for a long time, but they are expensive and do not all conform to one standard. For this reason they are not very common.

F   Magnetic tape is a cheap medium. You can use it to store very large amounts of data, but it does not allow random access. Every time you read or write a piece of data, you start at the beginning of the tape. Tape drives are slow. Therefore, it is only suitable for doing backups.

Task 8   Now exchange information with the other students in your group to complete all the sections of the table. Ask questions like these.

What are the advantages of floppy disks?
What are the disadvantages of magnetic tape?
Do CD-ROMs conform to a standard?

Study this example.

> *Magnetic tape is cheap, **but** it is very slow **because** tape drives are slow, **so** we use it only for backups.*

We use *but* to show a contrast, *because* to show that the next idea is a reason, and *so* to show a result. Other words and phrases used in this way are: *however* (contrast), *therefore* (result), and *for this reason* (result).

> *Magnetic tape is cheap. **However**, it is slow to use.*
> *Magnetic tape is slow. **Therefore**, we use it only for backups.*
> *Magnetic tape is slow. **For this reason**, we use it only for backups.*

Task 9 Fill in the gaps in this summary of storage devices using the correct word from this list.

but	however	because	so	therefore	for this reason

Floppies are very cheap, [1]_____ they are slow and have a limited capacity. Hard disks are fast and can store large amounts of data [2]_____ they are fixed inside the computer, [3]_____ you cannot use them to transfer data. You can transfer data with removable hard disks, [4]_____ they are expensive. CD-ROM disks can hold quite large amounts of data. [5]_____ , they are usually read-only [6]_____ you cannot change the information on them. Magneto-optical disks are like CD-ROMs [7]_____ you can write data on to them. They are removable and have large capacities, [8]_____ they are expensive and do not conform to a standard. [9]_____ , they are not very common. Magnetic tape is cheap and has a large capacity, [10]_____ it does not allow random access and drives are slow. [11]_____ it is only suitable for backups.

Problem-solving

Task 10 Study this description of one method of backing up your files.
Work in pairs to complete the table and answer the questions.

Establishing a comprehensive backup regime

Buy 10 tapes and label them Monday, Tuesday, Wednesday, Thursday,
Friday 1, Friday 2, Friday 3, Month 1, Month 2, Month 3.
　　For the first week, back up everything on each day to the
appropriately named tape, and on Friday, use Friday 1. In week 2,
do the same but use Friday 2, and in week 3 use Friday 3.　　　　5
　　In week 4, do exactly the same, but on Friday use Month 1. Do the
same for the next two months, but on the last Friday of each month,
use Month 2 and Month 3. Then start the whole cycle again.
　　With ten tapes, at any point in time you have full daily backups
for the last week, full weekly backups for the last month, and full　　10
monthly backups for the last three months.

Fill in the gaps in this table.

Tape	Label		Tape	Label
1	Monday		6	Friday 2
2	_____		7	_____
3	Wednesday		8	_____
4	_____		9	Month 2
5	_____		10	_____

Which tape do we use on these days?

1 Friday, Week 2   3 Thursday, Week 1   5 Friday, Week 8
2 Friday, Week 4   4 Monday, Week 2

Speaking

Task 11 Study how these terms are used in computing.

bit (b)　　a 0 or a 1 in the binary system
byte (B)　　a group of eight bits, e.g. 10101110
kilo (K)　　2^{10} (approximately a thousand)
mega (M)　　2^{20} (approximately a million)
giga (G)　　2^{30} (approximately a thousand million)

Now work in pairs, **A** and **B**. Fill in the gaps in this table as your partner
dictates. Ask your partner to repeat if necessary.

Storage device	Capacity		Storage device	Capacity
DVD	_____		CD-ROM	_____
High density floppy	_____		Large hard disk	_____
Average hard disk	_____		Tape	_____

Student A Your data is on page 118.
Student B Your data is on page 119.

9 Graphical User Interface

Tuning-in

Task 1   A Graphical User Interface (GUI) makes computers easier to use. A GUI uses icons. Icons are pictures which represent programs, folders, and files. Can you identify any of these icons?

Task 2   Find the icons for the software which controls these items.

1 date and time   3 fonts   5 a modem
2 the mouse   4 the keyboard   6 sounds

Listening: Dialog box

Task 3   Study this dialog box. Tick (✔) the features you can identify.

1 ☐ text box   3 ☐ checkbox   5 ☐ drop-down list box
2 ☐ tab   4 ☐ title bar   6 ☐ command button

Task 4   Now listen and check your answers.

Task 5   Listen again. Match the features of a dialog box (**1–4**) with the examples from the screen (**a–d**).

1 command button	a Find
2 dialog box	b Advanced
3 tab	c Look in
4 drop-down list box	d Stop

Task 6   Here are the steps for using this dialog box. Put them in the correct order.

a Enter name, location, and text required.
b Press Find Now command button.
c Choose tab.
d Open dialog box.

Reading: WIMP

Task 7   Study this screen display. Can you find these items?

1 a window	2 an icon	3 a pointer	4 a menu

Task 8   Find definitions in the text of these items.

1 menu	3 window	5 pointer
2 interface	4 active window	6 icon

Most computers have a Graphical User Interface. The **interface** is the connection between the user and the computer. The most common type of GUI uses a WIMP system. WIMP stands for Window, Icon, Menu (or Mouse), Pointer (or Pull-down/Pop-up menu).

Windows   A window is an area of the computer screen where you can 5 see the contents of a folder, a file, or a program. Some systems allow several windows on the screen at the same time and windows can overlap each other. The window on the top is the one which is 'active', the one in use.

Icons are small pictures on the screen. They represent programs, 10 folders, or files. For example, the Recycle Bin icon represents a program for deleting and restoring files. Most systems have a special area of the screen on which icons appear.

Menus give the user a list of choices. You operate the menu by pressing and releasing one or more buttons on the mouse. 15

The pointer is the arrow you use to select icons or to choose options from a menu. You move the pointer across the screen with the mouse. Then you click a button on the mouse to use the object selected by the pointer.

39

Language work: Making definitions

Study these descriptions of an icon.

> *An icon is a small picture on a computer screen.*
> *An icon represents items such as floppy disks.*

We can link these sentences to make a definition of an icon.

> *An icon is a small picture on a computer screen **which** represents items such as floppy disks.*

Study these other examples of definitions.

> *A mainframe is a very large computer **which** is used by universities, businesses, and government departments.*
> *A palmtop is a very small computer **which** can be held in one hand.*
> *A byte is a small unit of memory **which** can hold one character of data.*

Task 9   Add to the statements (1–10) using the extra information (a–j).

Example   *A barcode is a pattern of printed black lines which supermarkets use for pricing.*

1 A barcode is a pattern of printed black lines
2 A floppy is a disk
3 A motherboard is a printed circuit board
4 A password is a secret set of characters
5 A monitor is an output device
6 A disk drive is a unit
7 An expansion card is an electronic board
8 A CD-ROM drive is a common storage device
9 A notebook is a portable computer
10 The system unit is the main part of the computer

a it contains the main electronic components.
b it adds features to a computer.
c it is about the size of a piece of paper.
d supermarkets use them for pricing.
e it reads and writes to disks.
f it can hold 1.44MB of data.
g it allows access to a computer system.
h it controls all the other boards in a computer.
i it displays data on a screen.
j it reads data from a CD-ROM disk.

Task 10   Work with a partner. Ask for and make definitions of these items. Add other examples of your own.

1 PC	4 active window
2 menu	5 pointer
3 window	6 CD

Problem-solving

Task 11   Work in pairs. Study these forms the cursor can take on your computer. Try to match each icon to one item from the list below.

a   b   c   d   e   f   g

1 hourglass		**5** crosshair	
2 arrow pointer		**6** magnifying glass	
3 pointing finger		**7** drag and drop arrow	
4 not available			

Writing

Task 12   Write a description of the Shut Down Windows dialog box. Your description should answer these questions.

1   What does this computer screen show?
2   What do you use this dialog box for?
3   What features does the dialog box contain?
4   What happens if you click on each button?

10 Interview: Computing Support Assistant

Tuning-in

Task 1 Anne works in a large insurance company. She's a computing support assistant. She looks after people and their computers, and she helps with any problems people have. What sort of problems do you think they might have?

Listening

Task 2 Listen to Part 1 of the interview where Anne talks about the problems she helps with. Tick (✔) the problems she mentions.

1 ☐ paper jamming
2 ☐ finding options in programs
3 ☐ viruses
4 ☐ computer freezes
5 ☐ hard disk crashes
6 ☐ printer switched off
7 ☐ no paper in the printer
8 ☐ people forget their passwords
9 ☐ no toner in the printer

Task 3 Listen to Part 2 of the interview. Tick (✔) the ways Anne keeps up with new developments in computing.

1 ☐ reading books
2 ☐ reading computer magazines
3 ☐ speaking to other technicians
4 ☐ using the Internet
5 ☐ taking courses
6 ☐ trying programs herself
7 ☐ reading newspapers

Task 4 This table shows the number of hardware and software problems Anne had last year. Describe how often these problems happened, using the adverbs above.

Example   *There were sometimes problems with the network.*

Printers	116
Monitors	0
Cabling	13
Scanners	6
Network	34
Spreadsheet	15
Database	17
Word processing	93

Computing words and abbreviations

Task 5 Put the devices from the list into these sets.

Input	Output	Storage

CD-ROM disk   laser printer
digital camera   lightpen
dot-matrix printer   magneto-optical disk
fixed hard disk   magnetic tape
floppy disk   microphone
inkjet printer   monitor
joystick   removable hard disk
keyboard   scanner

Task 6 Match each definition (1–8) with the correct feature (a–h).

1 This is a window which appears when information about a choice is needed or when options have to be selected.
2 This indicates the amount of space between the dots which make up the image on a monitor.
3 This is part of a screen which is used to select an action, usually by clicking the mouse button over it.
4 This is a measure of the number of dots which make up the image on a monitor.
5 This shows a list of choices which the user can select from using the pointer.
6 This is part of a dialog box where the user can type file names and other information.
7 This is the speed at which the monitor refreshes the image on the screen.
8 This is a small picture on the screen which represents a program, folder, or file.

a	aperture grill pitch	e	drop-down list box
b	command button	f	maximum resolution
c	dialog box	g	refresh rate
d	icon	h	text box

Writing

Task 7 Answer these questions about the interview with full sentences. Then link your answers to make a short paragraph about Anne.

1 What kind of work does Anne do?
2 What does she like most about the job?
3 What kinds of problems do people have with hardware?
4 Why do computers freeze?
5 How does she keep up with new developments in computing?
6 What kinds of courses does she go on?

11 Networks

Tuning-in

Task 1 Study this example of a local area network (LAN). Answer these questions.

1 Who are the users?
2 What kind of hardware is used?
3 What do the doctors use it for?
4 What do the receptionists use it for?
5 What does the practice manager use it for?

**Newtown Health Centre
Local Area Network**

Task 2 Work in pairs. List some places where you might find a local area network.

Reading: Networks

Task 3 Study this diagram.
Then answer the questions.

1 What is a *network*?
2 What are its hardware components?
3 What is the difference between a *local area network* and a *wide area network*?
4 What advantages do you think networks have?

Task 4 Now read this text to check your answers to Task 3.

What is a network?

A network is simply two or more computers linked together. It allows users to share not only data files and software applications, but also hardware like printers and other computer resources such as fax.

Most networks link computers within a limited area – within a department, an office, or a building. These are called Local Area Networks, or LANs. But networks can link computers across the world, so you can share information with someone on the other side of the world as easily as sharing with a person at the next desk. When networks are linked together in this way, they are called Wide Area Networks, or WANs.

Networks increase productivity by allowing workers to share information easily without printing, copying, telephoning, or posting. They also save money by sharing peripherals such as printers.

Task 5 With the help of the diagrams on page 46 and the text above, identify these hardware components of the network.

1 _____ Most networks have at least one central computer which all the desktop computers connect to. This is the most important computer on your network. It stores the data files and application software programs that the users need to access or share with others.

2 _____ This is the desktop computer or notebook computer on your desk. It is linked to the server, and can access files and applications on it. Each computer on the network has a device called a network interface card which connects the computer to the network. Many computers come with these cards fitted as standard.

3 _____ Once you have a network you can share any number of these, including printers, scanners, CD-ROM drives, and backup devices.

4 _____ Desktops typically connect via telephone-type cabling to this intermediary device, which enables communication between servers and desktops.

Listening: Network topologies

Task 6 Study these diagrams. They show four network topologies. Try to match each diagram with the correct name.

| 1 ring | 2 bus | 3 star | 4 mesh |

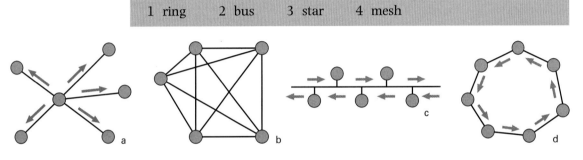

Task 7 Now listen and check your answers. The recording describes three topologies.

47

Task 8 Which topologies do these statements refer to?

1 If one of the computers fails, the whole network will be affected.
2 If we remove a computer from the network, it won't affect the other computers.
3 If the main cable fails, the whole network will fail.
4 If the central server fails, the whole network will fail.
5 If a cable breaks, the whole network will be affected.
6 If a computer fails, it won't affect the other computers.

Language work: Predicting consequences

The sentences in Task 8 predict the consequences of an action. For example:

The cable fails. The whole network will fail.
   (action)   (consequence)

If the cable **fails**, the whole network **will fail**.

Note that the action is in the Present simple, and the consequence in the *will* future.

Study these other examples.
If you don't use the right password, you won't get access to the network.
If you don't save your document, you will lose the information.

Task 9 Link each action (1–10) with a suitable consequence (a–j).

Example   *If you place a floppy disk near a magnet, you will destroy the data.*

1 you place a floppy disk near a magnet	**a**	the cursor moves to the left
2 you press Print Screen	**b**	the computer hangs
3 you input the correct password	**c**	it is not lost when you switch off
4 you add memory to a computer	**d**	you damage the drive
5 you move the mouse to the left	**e**	you copy the screen
6 you store data in RAM	**f**	you have access to the network
7 you use a faster modem	**g**	you destroy the data
8 there is a memory fault	**h**	it runs faster
9 you press the arrow key	**i**	your phone bills are lower
10 you move a CD-ROM drive with the disk in place	**j**	the cursor moves across the screen

---

Task 10 Complete these statements with a suitable action or consequence.

1 If you select the No button on the Shut Down Windows dialog box, ...
2 ... , you will close down Windows programs.
3 If you input the wrong password, ...
4 ... , your printer will not print.
5 If your monitor is too bright, ...

Problem-solving

Task 11 Study these rules for passwords. Then decide if the passwords which follow are good or bad. Explain your answers.

> **Network passwords**
>
> Usually you need a password to use a network. It is important to keep your password secret. The following rules make a password more difficult to guess.
>
> **Passwords** *should*:
> 1 be at least 6 characters long
> 2 have a mixture of numbers and letters
> 3 have a mixture of capital and small letters
> 4 be easy to remember.
>
> **Passwords** *should not*:
> 5 be a word from a dictionary
> 6 be a common name
> 7 include spaces, hyphens, dots, or symbols with a special meaning in computing, e.g. $, *, etc.

1 Colibarte	5 Eztv3xq
2 Tom3	6 Zuta.bal5
3 7Azab	7 4epilon
4 6Biscuit	8 Zabidon5

Writing

Task 12 Write a description of the LAN shown in Task 1. Use your answers to Task 1 to help you. Begin your description like this:

This LAN connects receptionists, doctors, and the practice manager in a health centre. It also connects the centre with the local health board.

12 Communications

Tuning-in

Task 1 Identify the different communications links between the office desktop in a San Francisco police station and the mainframe in Georgia State Police headquarters. Choose from this list.

1	fibre-optic cable	4	microwave transmission
2	earth-satellite transmission	5	satellite-earth transmission
3	telephone wire		

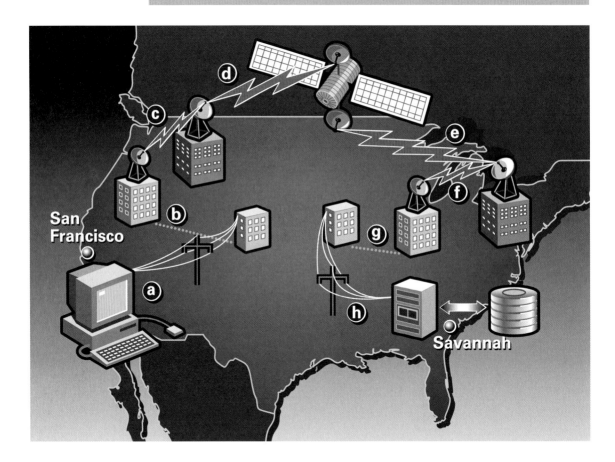

Task 2 Work in pairs. Try to think of other organizations which use long-distance computer communications to exchange information.

Listening: Voicemail

Task 3 Study this diagram of a voicemail system. Match each picture to the correct caption.

    a The digital message is stored in 'voice mailboxes' on disk.

    b The caller dictates the message.

    c When the recipient dials the mailbox, the message is converted back to analogue signals and delivered in audio form.

    d The message is converted from analogue to digital signals.

Task 4 Listen to this voicemail message from John Bailes in Brussels for Lenny Yang, a salesman with the Taytron company in London. Answer these questions.

    1 Which number does John Bailes dial to leave a message?

    2 What time was John's meeting with Lenny Yang?

    3 Why can't John meet at that time?

    4 How is John travelling to London?

    5 When does he leave Brussels?

    6 When does he arrive in London?

    7 Can he meet Lenny at 11.15?

    8 Why does Lenny have to email before 8.30?

Task 5 This is Lenny's appointments page on his PC. He checks his voicemail at 9.00. Is there any problem?

51

Reading: Video conferencing

Task 6 Study the instructions for using a video conferencing system. Try to find this information quickly.

1 What do these keys do?
   a (E)   b (L)   c (B)   d (H)

2 Which buttons do you use to:
   a make a call?   c switch off the picture-in-picture?
   b adjust the volume?   d zoom in and out the Near End camera?

Dialling a video call

Ensure 'PictureTel Ready' is displayed on the monitor.
Press the Call button (A). The monitor will prompt you to:

1 Make a manual call
2 Re-dial the last video numbers
3 Place a call from the speed dial menu.   5

To select a number from the speed dial list, use the direction keys (B),
then press Enter (C).

When the call has been successfully connected, you will see the
Far End location on the monitor.

Mute
On the left-hand side there is an audio mute key (E). When this is in   10
operation, a banner will appear on your main monitor telling you
that Near End, Far End, or both are on mute. Use the Mute button if
you want to have a private conversation.

Volume
To adjust the incoming volume, simply press the Volume key (F).

Picture-in-Picture
If you prefer not to see your own image, you can switch the P-I-P off   15
using button (G).

Moving the camera
The right-hand side of the keypad houses the Near End (I and J) and
Far End (K and L) camera controls. The diamond-shaped keys (I, K)
control the direction of the camera and (J, L) the zoom in and out.

Ending your video conference
When your meeting is finished, remember to end the call by pressing   20
the Hang Up key (H). It is preferable for the call originator to hang up.

Language work: Present passive

Study these steps in using the communications links to exchange data between San Francisco and Savannah, Georgia.

1 A police officer requests records of a suspect.
2 Her computer sends the message via lines and fibre-optic cable to a local microwave station.
3 The local microwave station transmits the request to the nearest earth satellite station.

Look at the active form – the agent is as important as the action.

*A police officer (= agent) **requests** (= action) records of a suspect.*

If we want to make the action more important than the agent, or if it is very clear who or what the agent is, we can say:

*Records of a suspect **are requested**.*

This is the Present passive form. We make this using *is* or *are* plus the *-ed* form of the verb (*requested, transmitted, relayed*). With irregular verbs, we use the irregular past participle form (*sent, given, spoken*).

Task 7   Fill in the gaps in these sentences. They describe how the police send a request from San Francisco to Savannah. Use the passive form of these verbs.

relay	request	send	transmit

1 Records of a suspect _____ .
2 The message _____ to a local microwave station.
3 The request _____ to the nearest earth satellite station.
4 The message _____ to a satellite in space.
5 The message _____ back to an earth satellite station.
6 It _____ to a microwave station.
7 It _____ via the telephone lines to the headquarters computer.

Task 8   Now describe how the records are sent from Savannah to San Francisco.

Problem-solving

Task 9   Work in pairs. Students in another country want to study the same computing course as yours without coming to your country. What communications links could your college or university use to make this possible?

Speaking

Task 10   Work in pairs. With the help of the rules provided, explain to your partner why these samples of handwriting are not easy for computers to read.

EWING 57320 Kent 5I3E4 9O6S LOOP

Student A Your rules are on page 118.   **Student B** Your rules are on page 119.

53

13 The Internet 1: email and newsgroups

Tuning-in

Task 1   Study this diagram of the Internet. With its help, match these definitions to the correct item on the diagram.

1   a device which selects the best route to send data from one network to another
2   a specialist computer which provides a service to a network
3   a company which provides Internet access
4   a large multi-user computer for processing very large amounts of data
5   computers connected together to share hardware and software

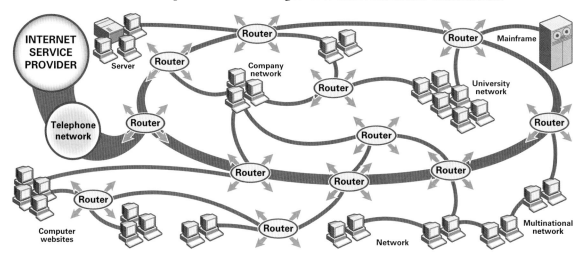

Task 2   Do you use the Internet? What do people use the Internet for? Make a list and discuss it with your group.

Listening: Email

Task 3   Study this email. Answer these questions.

1   Who is the sender?
2   What is his email address?
3   Who is it sent to?
4   What is it about?
5   What time was the message sent?
6   In what form is the main part of the message?

From: j.eastleigh@gltech.ac.uk
Date: 9/10/02, 15.35
To: gpark@ed.ac.uk, pricel@aol.com, aperez@kmc.ed.uk
Subject: Party

Dear all,
Too lazy to type. I've recorded this message as an attachment.
John

Task 4   Now listen to the attachment and find the answers to these questions.

1 When did he start his course?
2 Why is Friday different from other days?
3 Which class does he most enjoy?
4 What is he thinking of for a project?
5 Why does he not like the maths lecturer?
6 What sport does he play at lunchtime?
7 What's happening on the 17th?
8 Where will it be?
9 Who will be there?

Reading: Newsgroups

Task 5   You can exchange views on almost any subject by joining an Internet newsgroup. Which of these groups would interest the following people (1–6)?

a alt.algebra.help
b alt.asian-movies
c alt.comics.batman
d alt.education.disabled
e alt.fashion

f alt.sport.soccer.european
g alt.tasteless-jokes
h rec.antiques.bottles
i alt.food.wine
j alt.music.world

1 a football fan
2 a student with maths problems
3 a bottle collector

4 a comic book collector
5 a fan of Indian cinema
6 someone interested in clothes

Task 6   Study this exchange between subscribers to a newsgroup and find the answers to these questions.

1 What newsgroup is this?
2 Who sent the first message?
3 When did he send it?
4 Where was flight KN162 going?
5 What did the pilot see?

6 Who sent the second message?
7 What was the object?
8 Why do they think so?
9 What did the coastguard see?
10 What was he doing?

From: rsony@hotmail.com   Date: 06 March 1998 05.39
Newsgroup: alt.alien.visitors
The pilot of flight KN162 from Dallas to Fargo on February 17th 1998 reported a UFO heading north-east at an altitude of 10,000 metres and a speed of more than 2,000 km/h. He described the vessel as silver in colour, cigar-shaped and with short wings. Did anyone else see this?
Ron

From: Ben & Thelma   Subject: Re: UFO Report
This could be an experimental military plane. There are no reports of alien ships with wings. Most UFOs are saucer-shaped like the one which crashed at Roswell.

From: Steve   Subject: Re: UFO Report
Nonsense. Winged alien craft are quite common. US coastguard Harry Pitman saw 3 winged craft over Cape Cod on 4th March 1995 while searching for a missing fishing boat.

Language work:
Past simple vs Past continuous

We make the **Past continuous** with *was/were* + the *-ing* form of the verb. We often use it to provide the context for actions in the past.

> He **was flying** from Dallas to Fargo. He **saw** a UFO.
>   (action 1)   (action 2)

To show that one past action happened in the middle of another past action, we can link them using *when, as,* and *while.*

> He was flying from Dallas to Fargo **when** he saw a UFO.
> **As** he was flying from Dallas to Fargo, he saw a UFO.
> **While** he was flying from Dallas to Fargo, he saw a UFO.

We use the **Past simple** for completed actions, especially those which take very little time. We use the **Past continuous** to describe actions which happen over a period of time.

> He saw a UFO. It **was heading** north-east. It **was travelling** at 2,000 km/h.

Task 7   Put the verb in brackets into the **Past simple** or the **Past continuous**.

1 The plane _____ (go) to Fargo.

2 The UFO _____ (fly) at 10,000 metres.

3 The pilot _____ (notice) it had short wings.

4 The pilot _____ (report) the incident.

5 He _____ (describe) the vessel as silver in colour.

6 No one else _____ (see) the UFO.

7 The UFO _____ (head) north-east.

8 The coastguard _____ (see) three winged craft.

9 He _____ (search) for a missing fishing boat.

10 A UFO _____ (crash) at Roswell.

Task 8   Link these actions to show that one action happened during the other action. Put each verb in the correct tense, and use an appropriate time word: *while, as,* or *when.*

1 He _____ (fly) from London to Edinburgh. He _____ (see) a UFO.

2 Her computer _____ (crash). She _____ (search) the Internet.

3 They _____ (study). A fire _____ (start) in the Computer Lab.

4 She _____ (print) out her email. The printer _____ (develop) a fault.

5 They _____ (work) on the computer. Someone _____ (switch) on the power.

Problem-solving

Task 9 Study this typical email address. It belongs to Anna Lock, who works for the Pesto company in the UK.

userid   domain   type of organization   country

Study these examples of types of organizations and countries.

Organizations		Countries	
com or **co**	commercial organization	**at**	Austria
edu/ac	education	**au**	Australia
gov	government	**ca**	Canada
int	international organizations	**ch**	Switzerland
mil	military	**de**	Germany
net	network provider	**es**	Spain
org	not-for-profit	**fr**	France
	and other organizations	**it**	Italy

Whose email addresses are these? Match the addresses (**1–8**) to the list of users (**a–h**).

1 redcrossyouth@algonet.se
2 webmaster@fao.org.it
3 today@bbc.co.uk
4 jsmith@smith.senate.gov
5 rossi@cantsoc.com.it
6 sales@demon.net
7 lunchx@swto1.usace.army.mil
8 s.larrieu@ly.ac.fr

a a UN organization based in Italy
b a US politician
c a Swedish charity
d a student at a French university
e a news programme on a public broadcasting service in the UK
f an Italian wine co-operative
g a military organization based in the US
h an ISP

Writing

Task 10 Write a brief email to a friend describing your course. Your message should answer these questions.

1 What is your course called?
2 When do you have classes?
3 Which subjects do you study?
4 Which subjects do you enjoy most? Why?
5 Which subjects do you like least? Why?
6 What do you do in your free time?

14 The Internet 2: the World Wide Web

Tuning-in

Task 1 Work in groups. Study this extract from the Yahoo search engine home page (http://www.yahoo.com). Which category is the best one to search in for this information?

1 a new treatment for cancer
2 new Hollywood movies
3 the Italian word for *computer*
4 the main news stories in the US

5 the phone number of the White House
6 a video of a black hole developing
7 Tibetan Buddhism
8 unemployment statistics for Germany

YAHOO!®

Arts & Humanities
Literature, Photography...

Business & Economy
B2B, Finance, Shopping, Jobs...

Computers & Internet
Internet, WWW, Software, Games...

Education
College and University, K-12...

Entertainment
Cool links, Movies, Humor, Music...

Government
Elections, Military, Law, Taxes...

Health
Medicine, Diseases, Drugs, Fitness...

News & Media
Full Coverage, Newspapers, TV...

Recreation & Sports
Sports, Travel, Autos, Outdoors...

Reference
Libraries, Dictionaries, Quotations...

Regional
Countries, Regions, US States...

Science
Animals, Astronomy, Engineering...

Social Sciences
Archaeology, Economics, Languages...

Society & Culture
People, Environment, Religion...

Internet zone

Reading: Webpages

Task 2 Study these sample webpages. Classify them as:

1 news	2 sport	3 entertainment	4 education

Task 3   Now match each webpage to the correct text.

A   Offering unparalleled access to world news and current affairs, the Internet lets you keep up with the latest stories as they happen. Newspapers from around the world are available online, and TV news services, such as CNN (Cable News Network) and Sky TV, offer excellent coverage. There are even special interest news sites, including some designed for children.

B   Whatever your favourite sport, it is likely to have at least one devoted fan who has prepared a website dedicated to it. By visiting the site, you can pick up the latest news and gossip, and even chat to other fans around the world. As you might expect, football fans are well catered for on the Web with a mass of information on famous teams, league positions, fixtures, and player profiles.

C   Keeping up with your favourite band, finding out about exhibitions, or simply organizing your TV viewing is easy on the Web. Major TV companies have their own sites where you can find a wealth of information on TV shows and the activities of your favourite celebrities. If you want to find a restaurant, see a movie, or just visit a new bar, you will find the Internet a great resource.

D   You can study for school or college and even obtain a degree using the Internet. Universities from around the world have sites and some offer online courses. Most schools now have an Internet connection, and many schoolchildren use it for research and for keeping in touch with schools abroad. Children can also visit special online exhibitions created by world-famous museums.

Task 4   Look at this page from the CNN website. It contains a number of links labelled (**a–h**). Find the links which enable you to:

1 get the story behind the headline in full
2 post your own message about current events
3 search previous news stories for any reference you want
4 interact with other readers live using your keyboard
5 see the advertisement
6 change to Spanish
7 see the news in brief
8 watch videos of news stories.

Listening: Browser

Task 5   To download and read documents from the World Wide Web you need a software program called a *browser*. Study this section of a web browser screen. Identify these features.

| 1 title bar | 2 menu bar | 3 toolbar | 4 address box | 5 links |

Look more closely at the toolbar. Listen to the recording and try to identify which buttons are described.

Language work: *-ing* forms

Study these examples.

Keeping up with your favourite team is easy on the Web.
By visiting the site you can pick up the latest news.

We can often use the *-ing* form of verbs like nouns.

Browsing *the Web is popular.*
Some people like **shopping** *online.*

We use the *-ing* form after prepositions.

Without leaving *home you can visit any country on the Web.*
By clicking *on the link you can move to another page.*

Task 7 Complete each gap in these sentences with the *-ing* form of an appropriate verb from this list.

back up	become	enter	find	keep up	learn
link	receive	select	send	use	

1 _____ with the latest news on your favourite team is easy on the Web.

2 One of the most useful features of the Internet is _____ and _____ email.

3 The grandfather, father, son method is one way of _____ your documents.

4 Fibre-optic cable can be used for _____ computers in a network.

5 Search engines are ways of _____ information on the Web.

6 _____ a keyboard is the commonest way of _____ data into a computer.

7 _____ audio and video attachments is possible with email.

8 _____ a programmer means _____ a number of programming languages.

9 The White Pages are for _____ email addresses.

10 _____ an option in a menu is easy with a mouse.

Try to answer these questions using an *-ing* form.

Example   How do you draw pictures on a computer?
*By **using** a graphics package.*

How do you:

1 find a website?
2 select an option on a menu?
3 move rapidly through a document?
4 return to your starting page on the Web?
5 store favourite sites?
6 share ideas with other Internet users on a subject you're interested in?
7 increase the speed of your computer?
8 send voice and text messages to other Internet users?
9 end a search on the Web?
10 move the cursor round the screen?

Problem-solving

Task 9   Work in pairs. Decide which of the sites (**a–j**) to visit in order to find information on the following topics (**1–10**).

1 the latest scientific developments	**a** www.admarket.com
2 caring for your cat	**b** www.bubble.com/webstars/
3 calculating your tax	**c** www.buildacard.com
4 new cars	**d** www.carlounge.com
5 advertising on the Web	**e** www.encenter.com/ski/
6 books on sport	**f** www.petcat.co.uk
7 sending a virtual greetings card	**g** www.moneyworld.co.uk
8 economic data on Bulgaria	**h** www.newscientist.com/
9 your horoscope	**i** www.thebookplace.com
10 ski conditions in Europe	**j** www.worldbank.org

Writing

Task 10   Work in groups. Design a Web home page for your college or company. Write a headline with an explanatory paragraph about your college or company, and a menu which readers can choose from to find out more about different aspects of it.

Each member of your group should write a brief paragraph which readers can access when they click on one of the menu links.

15 Interview: Website Designer

Tuning-in

Task 1 Saladin designs websites. This is one of his designs. Discuss with your group what you think a good website should have.

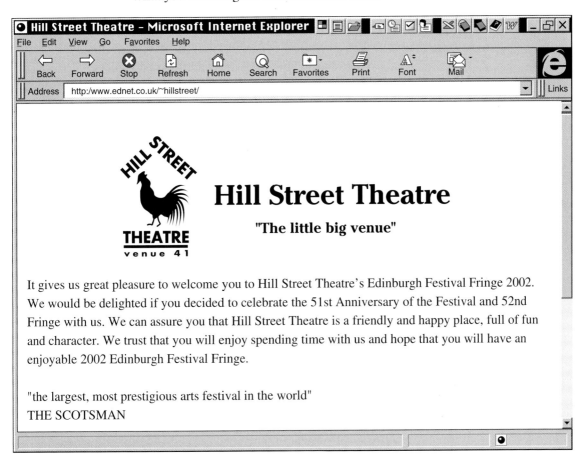

Listening

Task 2 In this interview Saladin describes what makes a good website. Listen to Part 1 of the interview and answer these questions.

1 Name two kinds of people who want websites.
2 Why is a website good for people with a lot of information to distribute?
3 What sort of clients is a website particularly useful for?
4 What does Saladin ask for first from a client?
5 What important point must be decided?
6 What must the client make a clear decision about?

Task 3 Listen to Part 2 of the interview and complete the five design principles mentioned.

1 There should never be _____ .

2 A maximum of _____ from home page to other pages.

3 Don't have _____ on one page.

4 Don't use multimedia simply to make _____ .

5 Remember there are still a lot of users with _____ .

Task 4 Listen to Part 3 of the interview. Decide which of these statements Saladin would agree with.

1 Information on websites should be divided into small sections.
2 Long sections can be a problem for users who want to print from a website.
3 It's a bad idea to have a lot of links to other sites.
4 You want users to bookmark your site as a way to get to other sites.
5 Your website should start with a brief piece of information to attract the reader.

Task 5 Now listen to the whole interview again. Put these pieces of advice about website design into two sets: **A** (things to do) and **B** (things *not* to do).

1 Include graphics only to make it look nice.
2 Divide information into small sections.
3 Have pages with dead-ends.
4 Have a lot of links to other sites.
5 Have a lot of links on one page.
6 Start with a brief piece of information to attract the reader.
7 Forget about readers with less sophisticated browsers.
8 Update your page regularly.

Language work: Indicating importance

We use *has/have to* and *must* to urge someone to do something because we feel it is important.

> You **have to/must** *put the keyboard directly in front of you.*
> You **mustn't** *type for hours without a break.*

We also use these words to show that something is required by a rule or law or by common sense.

> *The screen* **has to/must** *be easy to read.*
> *Noisy printers* **mustn't** *be too near.*

Task 6 Give advice about website design using *has/have to*, *must*, and *mustn't*. Use these answers to Task 5 to help you.

A: things to do

1 Divide information into small sections.
2 Have a lot of links to other sites.
3 Start with a brief piece of information to attract the reader.
4 Update your page regularly.

B: things not to do

1 Have a lot of links on one page.
2 Include graphics only to make it look nice.
3 Forget about readers with less sophisticated browsers.
4 Have pages with dead-ends.

Computing words and abbreviations

Task 7 Identify these abbreviations used in earlier units. Use the Glossary if necessary.

1 MB	3 ISP	5 PC	7 WAN	9 OCR
2 CD-ROM	4 LAN	6 RAM	8 SIMM	10 MHz

Task 8 Find terms related to these.

Example analogue signals – *digital signals*

1 bit
2 local area network
3 floppy disk drive
4 read-only memory
5 connector

Task 9 Find as many words as you know which go before or after these terms. You may use compound words.

Example disk: *disk drive, hard disk, floppy disk*

1 memory	3 mouse	5 key	7 monitor
2 printer	4 screen	6 cursor	

Writing

Task 10 Write a set of numbered points to advise someone thinking of designing a website. Advise them of things to do and not to do. Use your answers to Task 6, other information from the recording, and your own ideas.

How to design a website

1 _____
2 _____
3 _____
4 _____
5 _____

16 Word processing

Tuning-in

Task 1　General purpose packages such as word processors and spreadsheets have a number of features in common. Match these commands (**1–7**) to their meanings (**a–g**).

1	Open	**a**	alter data in the document
2	New	**b**	begin a new file containing no data
3	Save	**c**	alter the appearance of the text (e.g. change the font)
4	Print	**d**	start the application ready for use
5	Insert	**e**	enter information into the file
6	Edit	**f**	save the document to disk
7	Format	**g**	send the data to the printer to be printed out

Listening: Word processing screen

Task 2　Study this word processing screen. Can you identify these components?

1	Menu bar	5	Formatting toolbar
2	Insertion point	6	Standard toolbar
3	Status bar	7	Ruler
4	Title bar		

Task 3　Now listen to the explanation to check your answers.

Task 4　Number from **1** to **5** the features on the screen which allow you to:

1	insert a table	4	know which page you're on
2	print	5	underline part of a text.
3	change the font		

Reading: Draft letters

Task 5 Study these two drafts of a letter. Underline the changes made in Draft 2.

---

14 Glancey Street
Broadtown
EL12 4PQ
5th January 2003
Ms J Huckerby
Customer Services
Wanda Ltd.
Somerton
SP1 3QR

Draft 1

Dear Ms Huckerby

Re: Printer 6WL, Serial No 1563526

I purchased this printer from you in September, but it soon developed a fault. I sent it for repair under the guarantee on 19th November last year. It was returned on December 6th but it is still falty. I am returning it for further attention.

Yours sincerely

Paul Brandt

---

14 Glancey Street
BROADTOWN
EL12 4PQ

5th January 2003

Ms J Huckerby
Customer Services
Wanda Ltd.
SOMERTON
SP1 3QR

Draft 2

Dear Ms Huckerby

Re: Printer 6WL, Serial No 1563526

I purchased this printer in September, but it soon developed a fault. I sent it for repair under the guarantee on 19th November last year. It was returned on December 6th but <u>it is still faulty</u>. The paper jams every time it prints. I am returning it for further attention.

Yours sincerely

Paul Brandt

Task 6 Which of these word processing features has the writer used to make the changes in Draft 2?

Language work: Present perfect passive

Study this list of changes to Draft 2 of the letter in the **Reading** section.

1 tabs inserted
2 spelling checked
3 line spaces inserted
4 text justified
5 letters changed to capitals
6 words deleted
7 words inserted
8 words underlined
9 characters made bold

We can describe these changes like this.

   Tabs *have been inserted.*   The spelling *has been checked.*

The words in bold are in the **Present perfect passive**. We form the **Present perfect passive** with *has/have been* + *-ed* (the past participle of the verb). The **Present perfect passive** describes changes in the recent past which have a result in the present. Remember that we use the passive form if we want to focus on the action and not the agent, or if it is very clear who or what the agent is.

Task 7 Describe the other changes which have been made in Draft 2 in the same way.

Task 8 Now look at the two versions of this letter. Describe the changes which have been made in Draft 2.

Draft 1

ER Computing,
POB 305,
London

17th May

Dear Mr Hunt,

Thank you for your fax of the 14th and for your interest in the post of Computing Support Officer.

Before we can proceed with your application, we need a full CV together with the names of two referees.

Yours sincerely,

Sarah Gaites
Personnel Director

Draft 2

ER Computing,
POB 305,
London

17th May

Dear Ms Fellows,

Thank you for your letter of the 2nd and for your interest in the post of <u>Computer Programmer</u>.

Before we can proceed with your application, we need the names of two referees.

Yours sincerely,

Sarah Gaites,
Personnel Director

Problem-solving

Task 9 Study these pairs of words in different fonts from a desktop publishing package. Which font in each pair would be most suitable for an advertisement? Explain your choices. Use these phrases.

It's too ...
It's not ... enough.

Construction	ⲄⲟⲚSTⲢⲨⲤTⲓⲟⲚ
SOLICITORS	*Solicitors*
Wedding gowns	**WEDDING GOWNS**
Champagne	**Champagne**
Technology	𝔗𝔢𝔠𝔥𝔫𝔬𝔩𝔬𝔤𝔶

Writing

Task 10 Study these instructions for using the Find command.

1 Choose the Find command in the Edit menu.
2 Type the text you want to find in the Find What text box, for example, *present*.
3 Type the text exactly the way you want to find it.
4 If you want to find text that matches upper case and lower case with the way you type it, select Match Case.
5 If you want to find whole words only, select Find Whole Words Only. If not, you will find *presenting*, *represent*, *presenter*, etc.
6 Click on Find Next and the program will pause each time it finds the words you want.
7 The found text is highlighted on the screen.

Now write your own instructions for using Find and Replace based on this dialog box. Use your own examples.

Speaking

Task 11 Work in pairs, **A** and **B**. Explain to your partner in simple terms what you think are the functions of the labelled buttons on your copy of the standard toolbar.

Student A Your toolbar is on page 118.
Student B Your toolbar is on page 119.

17 Databases and spreadsheets

Tuning-in

Task 1 Study this example of a record from a database of company employees. What fields do you think it contains? What other fields might be useful?

Boot, Ronald	Marketing	Salesperson	30/5/68	£28,000

Task 2 Work in pairs. What fields would you include in a database for:

1 a national police computer?
2 a national driver and vehicle licensing centre?

Reading: Database search

Task 3 Study this simple database of volcanoes and answer the questions.

Name	Country	Continent	Height (m)	Status
Cotopaxi	Ecuador	South America	5978	active
Popocatapetl	Mexico	North America	5452	active
Sangay	Ecuador	South America	5410	active
Tungurahua	Ecuador	South America	5033	active
Kilimanjaro	Tanzania	Africa	5889	dormant
Misti	Peru	South America	5801	dormant
Aconcagua	Argentina/Chile	South America	6960	believed extinct
Chimborazo	Ecuador	South America	6282	believed extinct
Orizaba	Mexico	North America	5700	believed extinct
Elbrus	Russian Federation	Asia	5647	believed extinct
Demavend	Iran	Middle East	5366	believed extinct

1 How many fields are there?
2 How many records are there?
3 List the volcanoes in North America.
4 List the volcanoes over 6,000 metres.

Task 4 Read this text on database searches and answer the questions which follow.

Search

The 'search' facility allows you to look through the database for information. To do this, you must enter the field or fields that you want to search and the details that you want to find. This is called to *search on a field* using whatever *conditions* you require. To give an example, you might be looking for items in your database with 'height in metres greater than 5,000'. Here the field that you would be searching on is 'height in metres' and the condition you want is 'greater than 5,000'. The figure shows how a simple search on one field can be carried out.

```
                        Record Selection:
Name                          ⇧    equals                      ⇧
Country                            contains
Continent              (a)         begins with            (b)
Height in metres                   is greater than
Status                        ⇩    is greater than or equal to ⇩
```

Record Comparison Information: │

Selection Rules: Height in metres is greater than 5000

○ And ● Or
○ And ○ Or
○ And ○ Or
○ And ○ Or
○ And ○ Or

[Cancel]   [Delete Rule]   [Install Rule]   [Select](c)

1 What does box **a** contain?
2 What does box **b** contain?
3 Which selection rule is entered?
4 What is the function of button **c**?
5 How many records will this search find?

Task 5   What are the selection rules to find:

1 all active volcanoes?
2 all volcanoes over 6,000 metres?
3 all volcanoes in South America?
4 all active volcanoes in Ecuador?
5 all active volcanoes in South America higher than 5,500 metres?

Listening: Spreadsheet

Task 6   Study this extract from a spreadsheet for sales from a fast food outlet.
Answer these questions.

1 How many *columns* are there?
2 How many *rows* are there?
3 What is in *cell* A3?

	A	B	C	D	E
1	*Day*	*Food*	*Drink*	*Total*	*Profit*
2	Mon	385	92		
3	Tue	590	171		
4	Wed	547	106		
5	Thur		219		
6	Fri	1953	511		
7		2762			
8		1231	248		
9	TOTALS				

Study this table. Explain what each of the spreadsheet formulae (**1–5**) means.

Symbol	Meaning		Formulae
+	plus	**1**	= E3*15%
−	minus	**2**	= A10*B3
*	multiplied by, times	**3**	= SUM(B9:B24)
/	divided by	**4**	= K12/J12
=	equals, is equal to	**5**	= D4-B4
:	to		
%	per cent		

Example = *A2*B2* (formula)   *equals cell A2 multiplied by/times cell B2* (explanation)

Task 8 Listen to the recording. Fill in the gaps in the spreadsheet in Task 6 by entering the numbers, text, and formulae in the correct cells.

Language work: Certainty 1

We use *will* when we are certain one action will follow another.
> *If you switch on Caps Lock, you* **will** *get all capital letters.*

When we are less certain one action will follow another, we can use these expressions.
> *will probably/probably won't*
> *may (not), might (not)*
> *will possibly/possibly won't*

Task 9 In most databases you can use *wildcard characters* when you do not know exactly what you are searching for. Study these examples.

? any single character in this position
* any number of characters in this position
# a single number in this position
[ ] find these characters
[!] don't find these characters

Using these characters in a search, we can be certain what we will find and what we will not find.

Example *If you search for* **Sm?th***, you will find* **Smith** *and* **Smyth***, but you won't find* **Smit***.*

Write similar sentences for these searches.
1 Br?wn – Brown, Brawn, Braun
2 t*e   – tongue, the, tea, true
3 #th   – 12th, 4th, earth
4 Paul[ao] – Paul, Paula, Paulo
5 Mari[!a] – Marie, Maria, Mary

Complete these *If-* sentences using an appropriate expression of certainty.

Example   *If there is power failure, you* **may** *lose all your data.*

1 If there is power failure, you ————— lose all your data.

2 If you have a virus, it ————— corrupt your files.

3 If you don't back up your files regularly, you ————— lose some of them.

4 If you choose a simple password, someone ————— access your files.

5 If you don't give your files meaningful names, you ————— forget what they contain.

Problem-solving

Task 11 Some databases use symbols rather than words for selection rules. Here are some of the symbols and their meanings.

=	equals, equal to	<>	not equal to
=>	equals or greater than	.AND.	and
>	greater than	.OR.	or
=<	equals or less than	.NOT.	not
<	less than		

Study this extract from a database of members of a sports club, and the results of five searches. Write selection rules to obtain these results. Use the symbols above.

Example   Result – *Helen Trim* Selection rule – *Occupation = technician* .AND. Sex = F

First name	Surname	Sex	Age	Occupation
Lillias	Brown	F	21	student
Lucy	Cruden	F	28	actress
Alan	Brew	M	24	student
Helen	Trim	F	23	technician
John	Walls	M	26	student
John	Pond	M	31	computing officer
Arnold	Bright	M	31	technician

Search results

1 Lillias Brown, Alan Brew, John Walls
2 John Pond
3 Lillias Brown, Helen Trim
4 John Walls
5 Arnold Bright

Writing

Task 12 Go back to Task 2. Explain which fields you would include in a database for a national driver and vehicle licensing centre. Give reasons for each field.

18 Graphics and multimedia

Tuning-in

Task 1 Study this toolbox from a graphics package. Find the icons which represent these features.

1 text
2 eraser
3 polygon
4 rectangle
5 airbrush
6 select
7 curve
8 colour fill

Task 2 Work in pairs. List some occupations that use graphic design software, and say what they use it for.

Listening: Drawing a graphic

Task 3 Study these diagrams. They show the stages in the production of a simple graphic. Then listen to the recording and match each extract to the correct diagram.

1 ☐
2 ☐
3 ☐
4 ☐
5 ☐
6 ☐

a

b

c

d

e

f

Reading: Desktop publishing (DTP)

Task 4 Study this diagram which shows the software involved in producing a DTP document. Which software produced these parts of the final document?

1	page layout	4	bar chart
2	graphic	5	text
3	photograph		

Producing a DTP document

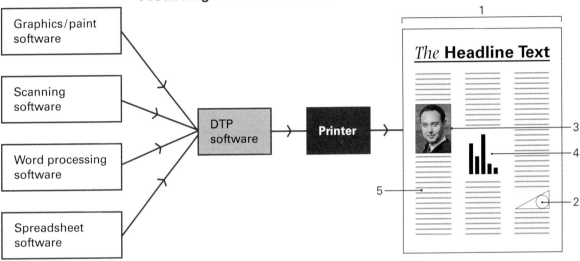

Task 5 Read Part 1 of the text. Then complete this table of the hardware required for DTP. Note down the reason for each choice.

Hardware required	Reason
Microcomputer with large hard disk and large amount of memory:	*graphics need a lot of memory space*
Laser printer	

Part 1 Desktop publishing (DTP) software allows the user to produce printout in the style of a newspaper. That is, in columns with pictures and other graphics. DTP is run on a microcomputer system with a laser printer for high quality, fast printout. The computer should have a large hard disk and a large amount of memory. A high resolution monitor with a 21-inch screen is recommended for easy working. A scanner is needed to import photographs and possibly a video digitiser to capture video images.

Task 6   Read Part 2 of the text to answer these questions.

1   What two computer applications does DTP integrate?
2   List the features that DTP software provides.
3   Why does it offer only basic word processing and graphics?

Part 2

DTP software can be thought of as integrated word processing and graphics, with additional features to enable pages to be laid out in columns and illustrations to be inserted. A facility to import photographs and video images is also provided. Often DTP software has only basic word processing and graphics facilities. It relies on the user making use of word processor and graphics software to prepare documents and illustrations before importing them into the DTP software. Its strength is in providing the structure to manipulate documents into columns or rows, and to cut and position graphics as required.

(line numbers: 5, 10)

Language work: Time clauses

Study these steps in the production of a graphic.

1   The basic design is drawn.
2   Detail is added.
3   Unnecessary parts are removed using the eraser.
4   The graphic is scaled to the right size.
5   The drawing is complete.
6   Colour is added.
7   Text is added.
8   The author works on the graphic.
9   The graphic is ready to print.
10   The finished product is printed.

We can link some of these steps using time words.

After and *before* indicate the sequence in which things happen.
For example:

    1 + 2   *After the basic design is drawn, detail is added.*
    3 + 4   *Before the graphic is scaled to the right size, unnecessary parts are removed using the eraser.*

When can indicate that one action happens immediately after another.
For example:

    5 + 6   *When the drawing is complete, colour is added.*

Until links an action with the limit of that action. For example:

    8 + 9   *The author works on the graphic **until** it is ready to print.*

Task 7 Study these steps in the production of a desktop-published student magazine.

1 Text is typed in using a word processor.
2 The text is edited.
3 The text is spellchecked.
4 Line drawings are made using a graphics package.
5 Photographs are scanned in with a scanner.
6 The first draft is completed.
7 The first draft is transferred to a page-makeup program.
8 Text and graphics are adjusted on screen.
9 They all fit together well.
10 The finished document is printed on a laser printer.

Link these pairs of sentences using these time words.

1 + 2 *after*	3 + 4 *after*	6 + 7 *when*	9 + 10 *after*
2 + 3 *before*	5 + 6 *after*	8 + 9 *until*	

Problem-solving

Task 8 Graphics packages allow you to:

> draw graphics   add text   change tools   change attributes
> scale the graphic   rotate the graphic

Which features have been used to change picture 1 to picture 2?

Writing

Task 9 Link these pairs of statements with suitable time words to make a description of the development of computers.

1 Electronic computers were developed.
  There were mechanical calculators similar in some ways to computers.
2 World War 2 started.
  The first electromechanical computer was developed to decipher codes.
3 The war ended.
  Bell Laboratories developed the transistor.
4 But it took more than ten years.
  Transistors replaced valves in computers.
5 Integrated circuits were introduced in the mid-1960s.
  Developments happened quickly.
6 The first microcomputers came on to the market in the mid-1970s.
  Desktop computing became a reality.

19 Programming

Tuning-in

Task 1 Work in pairs. The stages in programming (**1–7**) are listed below.
Fill in the gaps with the missing stages (**a–d**).

1 Analysing and defining the problem to be solved

2 _____

3 Coding

4 _____

5 _____

6 _____

7 Obtaining feedback from users

a Training the users

b Testing

c Designing the program

d Documenting

Task 2 Look at stage 1 of the list in Task 1. Discuss how you would analyse and
define the problem. Compare your ideas with other students in the class.

Listening: Flowcharts

Task 3 Programmers sometimes use flowcharts when planning a program.
Listen to Part 1 of the recording to identify these symbols used in flowcharts.

a _____ b _____ c _____ d _____ e _____

Task 4 Listen again to Part 1. This time write in each symbol a typical example of
an instruction often found there in flowcharts. Remember that one symbol
has no words.

Task 5 Listen to Part 2 of the recording which
describes this flowchart for calculating
sales tax. As you listen, fill in the gaps
where necessary.

Calculating sales tax

Input initial
cost (C)

YES

NO

Reading: Types of error

Task 6 Work in groups of three. Read one of the texts below and complete this table. When you have finished, exchange information with the others in your group to complete two similar tables.

Type of error	
Definition	
Example	
Ways to avoid or deal with this kind of error	

Text A

System errors affect the computer or its peripherals. For example, you might have written a program which needs access to a printer. If there is no printer present when you run the program the computer will produce a system error message. Sometimes a system error makes the computer stop working altogether and you will have to restart the computer. A sensible way of avoiding system errors is to write code to check that peripherals are present *before* any data is sent to it. Then the computer would warn you by a simple message on the screen, like 'printer is not ready or available'.

Text B

Syntax errors are mistakes in the programming language (like typing PRNIT instead of PRINT). Syntax errors cause the program to fail. Some translator programs won't accept any line that has syntax errors. Some only report a syntax error when they run the program. Some languages also contain special commands such as *debug*, which will report structural errors in a program. The programming manual for the particular language you're using will give details of what each error message means.

Text C

Logic errors are much more difficult to detect than syntax errors. This is because a program containing logic errors will run, but it won't work properly. For example, you might write a program to clear the screen and then print 'hello'. Here is a code for this:

```
10// Message        30  CLS
20  PRINT 'Hello'   40  END.
```

The code has a logic error in it, but the syntax is right so it will run. You can get rid of logic errors from simple programs by 'hand-testing' them or doing a 'dry run' which means working through each line of the program on paper to make sure it does what you want it to do. You should do this long before you type in the code.

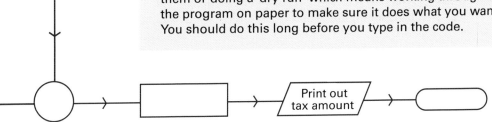

Print out
tax amount

Language work: Problem and solution

Study these ways of linking a problem and a solution.

> **Problem:** get rid of logic errors
> **Solution:** hand-test the program
>
> *You can get rid of logic errors **by hand-testing** the program.*
> ***To get rid of** logic errors, **hand-test** the program.*

Task 7 Match these problems and solutions. Link them following the examples above.

Problems	Solutions
1 connect a computer to a telephone line	a write code to check a peripheral is present before any data is sent
2 identify items for pricing	b use the *debug* command
3 add extra facilities to a computer	c add more memory
4 get more file storage space	d format the disk
5 find syntax errors	e use a removable disk
6 avoid marking the surface of a CD-ROM	f install an expansion card
7 improve the speed of your computer	g install a modem
8 avoid system errors	h fit a bigger hard disk
9 prepare a new disk for use	i use barcode labels
10 transfer information between computers	j hold it by the edges

Task 8 Suggest solutions to these problems. Then link the problem and your solution.

1 Make sure there are no viruses on a floppy disk.
2 Prevent unauthorized access to a network.
3 Avoid the risk of losing data.
4 Avoid eye-strain when using computers.
5 Avoid back problems when using computers.

Problem-solving

Task 9 Draw a flowchart for one of these activities. Then compare your completed flowchart with other students in your group.

- using a payphone
- planning a holiday
- choosing a new computer
- preparing for an important exam

Writing

Task 10 Read this description of the flowchart on page 78–9. Then write your own
description of the flowchart below.

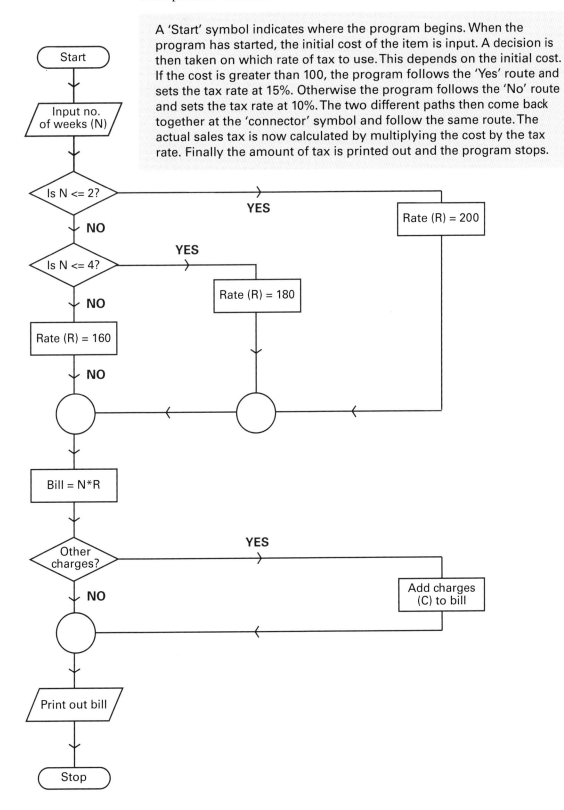

A 'Start' symbol indicates where the program begins. When the
program has started, the initial cost of the item is input. A decision is
then taken on which rate of tax to use. This depends on the initial cost.
If the cost is greater than 100, the program follows the 'Yes' route and
sets the tax rate at 15%. Otherwise the program follows the 'No' route
and sets the tax rate at 10%. The two different paths then come back
together at the 'connector' symbol and follow the same route. The
actual sales tax is now calculated by multiplying the cost by the tax
rate. Finally the amount of tax is printed out and the program stops.

20 Interview: Analyst/Programmer

Tuning-in

Task 1 Colin is an analyst/programmer. Study this screen display from one of his projects, Dante, and answer these questions.

1 What does Dante teach?
2 What kind of students is it for?
3 What do you think the calculator is for?
4 What happens if you get the answer wrong?
5 What happens if you get the answer right?

A building is on fire 5.4 km away.
The fire engine has gone 1.5 km.
How far is the fire now?

Listening

Task 2 In Part 1 of the interview Colin shows the fire engine page and subsequent pages to the interviewer. Listen and check your answers to Task 1.

Task 3 Listen to Part 2 of the interview and answer these questions.

1 What was the problem the programmers tried to solve with Dante?
2 What does the administrative package provide for the teacher?
3 What information does the program provide on use of the modules?
4 What does 'You can't debug your own code' mean?
5 Who tests the programs?
6 What do they try to do?
7 What problem did they have with graphics?
8 Colin discusses three types of error. What are they?

Listen to Part 3 of the interview and answer these questions.

1 Is programming stressful?
2 What does Colin do as a break from programming?
3 Where do the team do much of the design work?
4 How many people work with him?
5 What do they do?
6 How long did Dante take to write?
7 Why was it easy to split?
8 Tick (✔) the languages he mentions.

☐	C	☐	Visual Basic	☐	HTML
☐	C++	☐	JavaScript	☐	Delphi
☐	Basic	☐	Pascal	☐	Algol

9 How does he keep up with developments in his field?
10 Why does he hate to go home sometimes?

📟 **Task 5** Listen to the whole interview again. Tick the stages in the production of a program that Colin mentions.

1 ☐ Analysing and defining the problem   5 ☐ Coding
2 ☐ Designing the program   6 ☐ Testing
3 ☐ Training the users   7 ☐ Documenting
4 ☐ Obtaining feedback from users

Language work: Present simple vs Present continuous

Study these examples of the **Present simple** and the **Present continuous** from the interview with Colin. Which tense does Colin use for:
1 routines and procedures?
2 things happening now?
3 likes and dislikes which are always true?

Present continuous
*an example of what **we're working on** at the moment*
*there are three main areas **we're working in***
***I'm**, at the moment, **trying** to learn how to use Active Server pages*
***we're** now **using** a system called Visual Failsafe*

Present simple
*we **speak** to the users*
*we **offer** solutions*
*we **don't spend** a full day programming*
*we **go** to the canteen and **work** it **out***
*I **enjoy** my work*

We use the **Present simple** to describe routines, standard procedures, and things which are always true, such as likes and dislikes.
We use the **Present continuous** for actions going on at the moment.

Task 6 Complete these sentences by putting the verb in brackets into the Present simple or Present continuous.

1 At the moment I _____ (work) on a program for schools.

2 We always _____ (ask) the users, not the managers, what they need from the system.

3 Paul is a database expert so usually he _____ (do) anything on databases and I _____ (get) the interfaces.

4 We _____ (use) Active Server for this project because it's Web-based.

5 Commonly we _____ (use) C++ and JavaScript.

6 Whenever we _____ (finish) part of a project, we put a copy of the software in a sub-folder as a record.

7 I _____ (subscribe) to two magazines.

8 Right now I _____ (try) to learn how to use Active Server properly.

9 At the moment we _____ (develop) a Web-based project.

10 It's a magazine for people who know what they _____ (do).

Task 7 Write four sentences about any project you're working on at this moment, and about your daily routine.

Example *I'm working on a project about ...*   *I start classes each day at ...*
I'm designing a ...   *I finish at ...*

Computing words and abbreviations

Task 8 Sort these words about General Purpose Packages into these sets.

bold	cell	column	draw	field	fill	font
formula	justify	paint	record	rotate	row	scale
search	selection rules		sort	spelling checker		
tab	tool palette		underline			

Word processing	Databases	Spreadsheets	Graphics
_____	_____	_____	_____
_____	_____	_____	_____
_____	_____	_____	_____
_____	_____	_____	_____
_____	_____	_____	_____
_____	_____	_____	_____

Task 9   Verbs with prepositions are common in spoken English.

Example   *to work something out* = to solve a problem

Study these verbs with prepositions from this interview and earlier interviews. Try to use them in the correct form in sentences 1 to 10.

burn down	give up	come across	keep up with	come up
pick up	divide up	put out	find out	take up

1 If the fire engine doesn't arrive on time, the house will

   _____ .

2 I subscribe to magazines to _____ developments in programming.

3 In programming you often _____ the coding among a team of programmers.

4 If a site takes too long to download, people _____ and go to another site.

5 In the hardware class we _____ about things inside computers.

6 People may _____ your website by chance when they're browsing the net.

7 If you get the answer right, the fire engine _____ the fire.

8 When you test a program, different kinds of problems

   _____ .

9 Reading about new developments _____ a lot of Colin's free time.

10 He tries to _____ a copy of *Dr Dobb's Journal* when he can.

Speaking

Task 10   Work in pairs, **A** and **B**. Logic errors often occur when you are testing a condition before branching or exiting from a loop. Each of you has a short program which contains a logic error. Dictate your programs to each other line by line. Then together identify the logic error in both programs.

Student A Your program is on page 118.
Student B Your program is on page 119.

21 Languages

Tuning-in

Task 1 Study these sample sections of programs. Rank them from 1 (easiest to understand) to 5 (most difficult to understand).

a
```
TABLE FILE SALES
SUM UNITS BY MONTH BY CUSTOMER
ON CUSTOMER SUBTOTAL PAGE  BREAK
END
```

b
```
10101001  01000010  00010100
11101110  11111111
```

c
```
REPORT THE BASE SALARIES
BROKEN DOWN BY REGION
FOR MANAGERS IN ENGLAND
```

d
```
mov  ah, 3Dh
mov  al, 0
push  cs
pop  ds
```

e
```
A=0
X=1
INPUT Y
FOR X=1 TO 3
A=Y**X
PRINT A
NEXT X
END
```

Task 2 Here is a list of language types used by programmers ranked from natural human language at the top to machine code at the bottom. Can you match any of the samples in Task 1 to this list?

1 Natural language
2 Very high-level language
3 High-level language
4 Assembly language
5 Machine code

Listening: A Basic program

Task 3 Study this fragment of a Basic program. What do you think this program is for?

```
 10   REM AVERAGES
 20
 30   PRINT 'TYPE 999 TO INDICATE END OF DATA'
 40
 50   SUM = 0
 60
 70   PRINT 'PLEASE ENTER A NUMBER'
 80
 90   DO WHILE NUMBER <>999
100
110   COUNTER = COUNTER + 1
120
130   INPUT NUMBER
140
150
160   PRINT 'THE AVERAGE OF THE NUMBERS IS:' ; AVERAGE
170
```

Task 4 Now listen to the recording to complete the missing lines in the program.

Task 5 Study the completed program. It contains three faults. Can you find them?

Reading: Computing languages

Task 6 Work in groups of three. Read two of the texts about computing languages and make notes in the table on page 88. Then exchange information about the other texts with other students in your group.

C++ was developed from the C language. It was designed as a systems programming language with features that make it easy to control the computer hardware efficiently. It was used to produce the Microsoft Windows operating system. It is portable, i.e. programs written in C++ can be easily adapted for use on many different types of computer systems.

HTML stands for HyperText Markup Language. It is a page description language used for creating webpages. HTML uses a system of tags to mark page links and formatting. For example, the tag <u> tells the program to start underlining a text. Although programs cannot be created using HTML, small programs can be embedded in HTML code using a scripting language like JavaScript.

Java is a programming language originally designed for programming small electronic devices such as mobile phones. It can run unchanged on any operating system that has a Java Interpreter program. Java is used for writing programs for the World Wide Web.

JavaScript is a scripting language. It is powerful and easy to use. Scripts are small programs that can be used to perform simple tasks or tie other programs together. JavaScript is designed for use inside webpages. It can enable a webpage to respond to a mouse click or input on a form. It can also provide a way of moving through webpages and produce simple animation.

Visual Basic is a programming environment, not simply a language. It uses the language BASIC, a simple language developed to make it easy for people to learn how to program. Visual Basic has predefined objects such as dialog boxes, buttons, and text boxes which can be chosen from a toolbox and dragged across the screen using the mouse and dropped into the required position. BASIC programming code is attached to form a complete program. Visual Basic is used to write general purpose applications for the Windows operating system.

Delphi is similar to Visual Basic. It is also a programming environment for developing programs for the Windows operating system. It has predefined objects that can be chosen from a toolbox. In Delphi, however, the code attached to the objects is written in a form of Pascal. You can think of Delphi as a kind of 'Visual Pascal'. Like Visual Basic, it is often used for general purpose programs.

Language	Associated language	Type of language	Use
C++	_____	_____	_____
HTML	_____	_____	_____
Java	_____	_____	_____
JavaScript	_____	_____	_____
Visual Basic	_____	_____	_____
Delphi	_____	_____	_____

Task 7 Now read the texts again and answer these questions about special features of the languages.

1 Which language uses a system of tags?
2 Which languages are designed to be used inside webpages?
3 Which language was used to write the Windows operating system?
4 What is a 'portable' language?
5 Which language can have small programs embedded in it using JavaScript?
6 What does HTML stand for?
7 Which languages can only be used in the Windows operating system?
8 Which language cannot be used for writing programs?

Language work: Reporting screen messages

Study these examples of screen messages. Note how we report them.

Please enter a number.	**It requests you to** *enter a number.*
Type 999 to indicate end of data.	**It tells you to** *type 999 to indicate the end of the data.*
Do not attempt to log on.	**It tells you not to** *attempt to log on.*
Printer out of paper.	**It informs you that** *the printer is out of paper.*

Study these examples of screen messages. Note how we report them.

Do you want to exit (Y/N)?	**It asks you if** *you want to exit.*
What is your password?	**It asks you what** *your password is.*
How many copies do you want to print?	**It asks you how many** *copies you want to print.*

Task 8 Report each of these screen messages.

1 Make sure printer is switched on before continuing.
2 System halted.
3 Press any key to continue.
4 Please type next number.
5 Do not proceed.
6 Please choose from menu below.
7 Non-system disk in drive a.
8 Paper jam.

Task 9 Report each of these screen messages.

1 Continue (Y/N)?
2 What is the drive letter of your hard disk?
3 Are you sure you want to copy the selected files?
4 Do you want to virus check another disk?
5 Is the printer ready?
6 In which directory do you want to install the program?
7 Delete files (Y/N)?
8 Are you sure you want to shut down the computer?

Problem-solving

Task 10 Using the information in the reading texts and the table in Task 6, decide which languages would be best for these users and tasks.

1 A language for school pupils learning to program for the first time.
2 A language for professional programmers who want their software to run on any type of computer system.
3 A language for a student who wants to create her own webpage.
4 A language for a website designer who wants to include simple animation in a site.
5 A language for computing students who want to write a general purpose program as a college project.

Writing

Task 11 Look back at the notes you made in the table in Task 6. Write a brief summary of the reading texts based on your notes.

Language	Associated Language	Type of Language	Use
C++	C	Programming	General and systems programming

Example *C++ is a programming language. It is used for general and systems programming.*

22 Low-level systems

Tuning-in

Task 1 Label this diagram of a computer system with these terms.

storage	input	output	processor	ROM

For example:
keyboard,
mouse,
lightpen,
scanner

For example:
monitor,
printer,
plotter,
speaker,
motor

For example:
hard disk, floppy disk, CD-ROM

Task 2 Work in pairs. What other examples of input devices, output devices, and storage devices can you add to the diagram?

Listening: The CPU

Task 3 Study this diagram of the Central Processing Unit. Answer these questions.

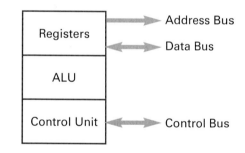

1 What does ALU mean?
2 What is a *register*?
3 What does the *control unit* do?

Task 4 Listen to Part 1 of the recording. Check your answers to Task 3.

Task 5 Listen again to find the answers to these questions.
1 What sort of functions does the ALU perform?
2 Name a logic operation performed by the ALU.
3 Which part of the CPU controls printers?
4 What is the difference between registers and main memory?

Task 6 Look at the diagram in Task 3 again. Try to answer these questions.
1 What is the function of buses?
2 Which buses are *bidirectional*?
3 What kind of information is carried by the data bus?
4 What does *unidirectional* mean?

Listen to Part 2 of the recording. Check your answers to Task 6. Then complete this table.

Bus	Uni/Bidirectional	Links
Data	_____	_____
Address	_____	_____
Control	_____	_____

Reading: The machine cycle

Task 8 Study this diagram of the machine cycle. Answer these questions.

1 How many steps are there in the machine cycle?
2 What are the *Fetch* and *Decode* steps together called?
3 Which steps together are called *E-time?*
4 Where does the *Decode* step happen?

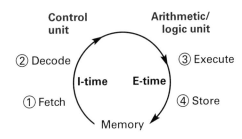

Task 9 Read this text quickly to check your answers to Task 8.

How the CPU executes program instructions

Let us examine the way the central processing unit, in association with memory, executes a computer program. Many personal computers can execute instructions in less than one-millionth of a second, whereas supercomputers can execute instructions in less than one-*billionth* of a second. ⁵

Before an instruction can be executed, program instructions and data must be placed into memory from an input device or a secondary storage device. The data will probably make a temporary stop in a register. As Figure 1 shows, once the necessary data and instruction are in memory, the central processing unit performs the ¹⁰ following four steps for each instruction:

1 The control unit *fetches* (gets) the instruction from memory.
2 The control unit *decodes* the instruction (decides what it means) and directs that the necessary data be moved from memory to the arithmetic/logic unit. These first two steps together are called ¹⁵ *instruction time*, or *I-time*.
3 The arithmetic/logic unit *executes* the arithmetic or logical instruction. That is, the ALU is given control and performs the actual operation on the data.
4 The arithmetic/logic unit *stores* the result of this operation in ²⁰ memory or in a register.

Steps 3 and 4 together are called *execution time*, or *E-time*. The control unit eventually directs memory to release the result to an output device or a secondary storage device. The combination of I-time and E-time is called the *machine cycle*. ²⁵

Task 10 Read the text again to find the answers to these questions.

1 What must be put into memory before an instruction can be executed?
2 Where will the data be stored temporarily?
3 What operation does the control unit perform on the data?
4 Where does the ALU store the results of its operations?
5 What happens to the results eventually?
6 What is the machine cycle?

Language work: Contrast

Study these pairs of statements.

1 *The data bus is bidirectional.*
  The address bus is unidirectional.

2 *Registers hold data immediately required.*
  Main memory stores data required in the near future.

3 *PCs can process in a millionth of a second.*
  Supercomputers can process in a billionth of a second.

Each pair contains a contrast. We can show this by linking them as follows:

1 *The data bus is bidirectional,* **whereas** *the address bus is unidirectional.*
2 *Registers hold data immediately required.* **In contrast**, *main memory stores data required in the near future.*
3 *PCs can process in a millionth of a second,* **but** *supercomputers can process in a billionth of a second.*

Task 11 Link each of these pairs of contrasting statements using *whereas, in contrast,* or *but.*

1 Dot matrix printers are noisy. Laser printers are quiet.
2 Floppy disks store small amounts of data. Hard disks store large amounts of data.
3 Handheld computers fit into your pocket. Supercomputers occupy a whole room.
4 High-level languages are easy to understand. Machine code is very difficult to understand.
5 BASIC is a simple language. C++ is complex.
6 Modern computers are powerful and relatively cheap. Older computers were less powerful and quite expensive.
7 An analyst analyses problems and finds solutions. A programmer turns these solutions into computer programs.
8 A graphics package produces images and designs. A word processor produces texts.

Problem-solving

Task 12
Work in pairs, **A** and **B**. Explain to your partner how to convert a number from one system to another. You can write down the steps and show them to your partner, but you must explain each step in English.

Student A Your conversion is on page 118.
Student B Your conversion is on page 119.

Writing

Task 13
Describe how an interrupt works by linking these pairs of sentences using suitable time words.

1 A printer runs out of paper.
   An interrupt carries a signal to the CPU.

2 The CPU receives the signal.
   The CPU interrupts its tasks.

3 The CPU saves its current status in a special area of memory.
   The CPU sends a message to the user.

4 The user reloads the paper tray.
   The processor returns to its previous state.

23 Future trends 1

Tuning-in

Task 1 Smart cards, robotics, and virtual reality are three areas of computing where developments are taking place very fast. Working in groups, try to add to these lists of current and possible future applications.

Smart cards	Robotics	Virtual reality
identification	welding cars	games
high-security access	repairing nuclear power plants	virtual travel
electronic money	bomb disposal	

Listening: Virtual reality

Task 2

Listen to Part 1 of this recording. Complete the gaps in this table of equipment required to use virtual reality.

Equipment	Alternative name	Purpose
_____	head-mounted display	_____
VR glove	_____	makes your hand feel pressure
VR mouse	_____	_____

Task 3

Listen to Part 2. Make a note of the existing and possible future uses of virtual reality which are mentioned.

Existing uses	Possible future uses
_____	_____
_____	_____
_____	_____

Reading: Future developments

Task 4

Work in groups of three, A, B, and C. Read one of these texts on developments in computing, and make notes in the table below.

Development	_____
Application/s	_____
How soon?	_____

Text A

SMART CARDS
A chip to save your life

If your friend suddenly had an accident and was unconscious or incoherent, could you provide any information to an ambulance crew? Would you know her blood type, her allergies, the prescription drugs she takes? Probably not. Even family members may not have this information, or be too distraught themselves to provide needed medical information. Enter the MediCard, a plastic card that has an embedded chip containing all that patient information. Small computers that can read the cards are installed in ambulances and in hospital emergency rooms. This system is working successfully in some communities. The biggest problem is making sure that people carry their cards at all times.

5

10

Text B

ROBOTICS
What is a micro-machine?

One of the most important steps in computing technology in the coming years is likely to be a return to mechanical methods. Using the same process used to create chips, it's possible to fabricate mechanical parts – levers, gear wheels, and small motors.

The best known example of a micro-machine was created by Sandia Laboratories in New Mexico in the US. It's a complete motor developing 50μW of power in one square millimetre – still a bit big for some of the micro-machines planned for the future. 5

What are micro-machines going to be used for? Obvious applications are sensors, gyros, and drug delivery. The idea is that a micro-machine could have a strain sensor or a gyroscopic attitude sensor and electronics built into a single chip-sized package. The idea of using a micro-machine to deliver drugs is getting a bit closer to more sci-fi applications. Only a step further is the idea of building insect-sized robots that could do difficult jobs in very small places. Swallowing an ant-sized machine to cure you or putting one inside some failed machinery seems like a really good idea! 10 15

Text C

VIRTUAL REALITY
Getting practical

Here are some applications of virtual reality under development. Wearing head mounts, consumers can browse for products in a 'virtual showroom'. From a remote location a consumer will be able to manoeuvre and view products along rows in a warehouse. Similarly, from a convenient office a security guard can patrol corridors and offices in remote locations. 5

Air traffic controllers may someday work like this. Microlaser scanner glasses project computer-generated images directly into the controller's eyes, immersing the controller in a three-dimensional scene showing all the aircraft in the area. To establish voice contact with the pilot of the plane, the controller merely touches the plane's image with a sensor-equipped glove. 10

Using virtual reality headsets and gloves, doctors and medical students will be able to experiment with new procedures on simulated patients rather than real ones. 15

Task 5 From your notes, explain what you have read to other students in your group.

Language work: Making predictions

Study these predictions.

Many more people will use the Internet.
Doctors will experiment with new procedures on simulated patients.
Micro-machines are going to be used for drug delivery.

We can use *will* and *is/are going to* to make predictions about things we are confident will happen.

Task 6 Make predictions about these things.

1 the number of PCs in use
2 the power of computers
3 the capacity of storage devices
4 the size of computers
5 the use of smart cards
6 the use of mainframes
7 robots and housework
8 computers and cars
9 wearable computers
10 the price of computers

Problem-solving

Task 7 What kind of information would you encode in the following smart cards?
Compare your answers with other students in your group.

1 a medical card
2 an identification card
3 a sports club membership card
4 an electronic wallet

Writing

Task 8 Study this graphic which shows how a smart card system could be used in a
college, or other large organization. Use it to write a report recommending
that your institution or company introduce a smart card system.

Start like this: *A student/company smart card can be used in many ways. It can be
used as a key to the building. Only cardholders can open the doors.*

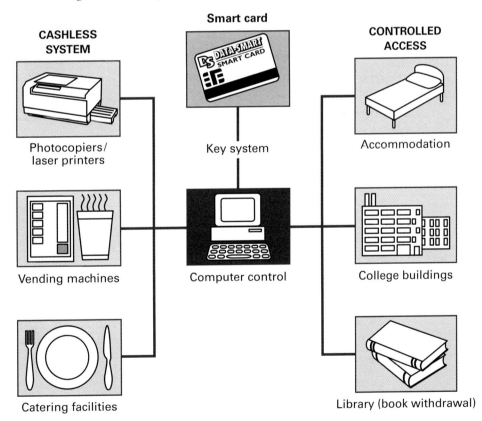

CASHLESS SYSTEM

Photocopiers/laser printers

Vending machines

Catering facilities

Smart card

Key system

Computer control

CONTROLLED ACCESS

Accommodation

College buildings

Library (book withdrawal)

24 Future trends 2

Tuning-in

Task 1 Study these predictions. Tick (✔) those you agree with and cross (✘) those you disagree with.

2004   Three-dimensional fax ☐

Computer touch screens which unfold from your wristwatch ☐

2005   Computers which write their own software ☐

2007   Smart clothes which change their thermal properties depending on the weather ☐

2010   Robots for guiding blind people ☐

2012   One-Petabit memory chip ☐

2013   Artificial intelligence which imitates the brain ☐

2015   Artificial lungs ☐

2020   Regular manned flights to Mars ☐

2030   Direct connections between brain and computer ☐

2035   Artificial brain ☐

Task 2 Compare your answers with other students in your group. Explain why you agree or disagree with these predictions.

Listening: Schooling of the future

Task 3 Study this diagram which shows how school children may benefit from IT developments in the 21st century. Answer these questions.

1 What hardware will school pupils have?
2 What will be the role of the *cybersage*?
3 What will be installed alongside video games in arcades?
4 What will Internet links allow children to do?
5 How will school project work benefit?

Homes
Learning at home will become easier and more important.

Amusement arcades
Video games operate alongside Internet terminals.

Town halls
Live access to local officials.

Internet provider

Palmtop computers
All children will use them. They will be connected to the school's network and the Internet, and enable pupils to use email.

Universities
Live connection to classes and lectures will be possible.

Schools
Using the Internet will increase paper-free learning.

Schoolwork can be integrated with nationwide research. Children will be able to communicate directly with experts. A *cybersage* will be on call to help with problems or provide information.

Task 4 Listen to Part 1 of the recording. The speaker argues in favour of these developments. Note down the main points she makes.

Task 5 Listen to Part 2. The speaker argues against these developments. Note down the main points she makes.

Task 6 Now listen to the whole recording. What reasons do the speakers give for each of their main points?

99

Reading: Future trends

Task 7   Work in groups. Predict how computers will affect our future lives in one of these areas – health, shopping, or money.

Task 8   Work in groups, A, B, and C. Read one of these texts on the impact of computers on one aspect of daily life. Make notes in the table below.

Development	Date	Details

Text A

HEALTH
Body chips

In the next decade we can have miniature computers inside us to monitor, and even regulate, our blood pressure, heart rate, and cholesterol. Such a chip would include a microprocessor, sensors, and a radio frequency device that would permit accurate read-outs of vital statistics. All this would happen, of course, without taking   5
any blood or attaching any external devices to the body.

Since we are already familiar with the notion of an internal pacemaker for the heart, including a chip or two may not seem all that astonishing. But this is just the beginning. Experts foresee, within twenty years, implanted chips that can correct our ability to   10
interact with the world. Once implanted, the chip is invisible, unlike a hearing aid. A more common implant would be a chip to correct visual signals. No more glasses!

Text B

SHOPPING
Computer shopping

This may sound very much like shopping by the Internet, but in fifty years' time it will be very different. Shoppers will be able to scan down virtual supermarket aisles on their PC and click on to whatever they want; the goods will then be delivered shortly afterwards. Customers may well be able to call up a virtual assistant who will   5
talk them through their shopping or to ask the computer for suggestions. Moreover, people will be able to get background information on shops and goods, and will be able to boycott any that offend their ethical considerations.

Text C   **MONEY**
              Electronic cash

Bank customers can now download money from their account to an
electronic wallet, a smart card, using a specially designed phone
equipped with a smart card reader. To download cash you have to
enter your PIN. You can then use your electronic wallet to pay for
goods and services, to purchase goods across the Internet, and to   5
transfer money to other cardholders.

Using the Internet, customers can now check their account
balance and see their latest statement. One bank has developed a
multi-currency payment engine which allows online retailers to sell
their goods in sixteen countries, with customers paying in their local 10
currency. With these developments, coins and notes are likely to
disappear.

Language work: *will* and *would*

Compare these examples of predictions.

> A bodychip **will include** a microprocessor.
> A bodychip **would include** a microprocessor.

> A common implant **will be** a chip to correct visual signals.
> A common implant **would be** a chip to correct visual signals.

We use *would* as a 'less definite' form of *will* when we make predictions.
Often we imply that something else must happen first. For example:

> A body chip **would include** a microprocessor. *(first we have to develop
> body chips)*
> The National Grid **would link** all schools and colleges. *(first we have to
> make sure there is enough money to make it happen)*

Task 9   Link these words to make predictions with *would*.

1 computers / write / own software
2 implants / stimulate / muscles of disabled
3 screen / unfold / wristwatch
4 clothes / alter / thermal properties
5 robot pets / require / no food
6 artificial lungs / help / cancer patients
7 people / be able to / travel to Mars
8 a body chip / correct / poor vision

Task 10 Study these notes about a possible 'cybercity' of the future. Make each set of notes into a prediction using *would*.

1 fibre-optic links between every house
2 paper-free education
3 no money used
4 computers in every house
5 driver-less public transport
6 wall-size computer screens for entertainment
7 houses cleaned by robots
8 virtual doctors for medical advice

Task 11 Work in pairs. Write other predictions of your own about the cybercity.

Speaking

Task 12 Work in pairs, **A** and **B**. Explain to each other a new development which may replace passports at border controls.

Student A Your information is on page 118.
Student B Your information is on page 119.

Problem-solving

Task 13 In groups, discuss how future developments in computing could help solve the problems of people who:

1 cannot hear
2 cannot see
3 cannot use their arms and legs.

Compare your ideas with the rest of the class.

25 Interview: IT Manager

Tuning-in

Task 1 Which do you think came first in the development of computing?

1 The first computer or the first transistor?
2 Integrated circuits or the first minicomputer?
3 The first IBM PC or the first Apple Macintosh?

Check your answers using this data on the development of computing.

Computer generation	Dates	Technology
First	1951–58	vacuum tubes (valves)
Second	1958–64	transistors
Third	1965–70	integrated circuits (ICs)
Fourth	1971–	microprocessors

1942	First electronic computer built
1947	Transistor invented
1954	First commercial computer put on sale
1960	First minicomputer
1965	ICs introduced
1971	Microprocessors introduced
1981	First IBM PC
1984	First Apple Macintosh
1993	First palmtop developed

Task 2 Work in pairs. What do you think will be the next important developments in computing? Make a list.

Listening

Task 3 Tom is head of IT in a large company. In Part 1 of the interview he talks about past developments in his own company. Listen and fill in the gaps in this table.

Date	What happened
_____	Started in computing. Transistorized computer
1974	_____
1980	_____
_____	Enormous changes in hardware
_____	Change from central to distributed computing
early 90s	_____

⊟ Task 4   Listen again to find the answers to these questions.

1 How big a memory did the ICT 1904 have?
2 What kind of drive did it have?
3 By how much did electrical load drop each year?
4 Why did it drop?
5 What changes were there in staffing?
6 What was the problem with hardware in the early days?

⊟ Task 5   Listen to Part 2 of the interview. Tick (✔) the statements which match Tom's views. Cross (✘) those which do not.

1 ☐ Speech recognition will be important.
2 ☐ Users will use a web interface to access programs.
3 ☐ Unless there's a good reason for it, people will not want to change because computers already do most things they want.
4 ☐ New products provide significant changes.
5 ☐ Things will get cheaper and faster.
6 ☐ Video conferencing is worthwhile for long distances.
7 ☐ Computer teaching is good for reinforcing, practising, and self-study.
8 ☐ Computers will replace teachers.

Language work: Certainty 2

Study these predictions from the interview. Which predictions is Tom most certain about?

We're going to live in the web browser environment a lot more.
Things will get cheaper and faster.
I think speech recognition could be big.
Computer teaching may be used more.
I don't see computer teaching replacing courses.

Study these ways of showing how certain you are about future events.

Certain	Fairly certain	Uncertain
YES *will happen* *is/are going to happen*	*I think it will happen.* *It will probably happen.*	*It may happen.* *It could happen.*
NO *will not/won't happen* *is/are not going to happen*	*I don't think it will happen.* *It's unlikely to happen.* *I don't see it happening.*	*It might happen.* *It's a possibility.*

Task 6   Do you think these developments will take place in the next ten years? Give your own views using the expressions listed opposite.

1 Computers will replace teachers.
2 Computers will direct surgical operations.
3 Computers will replace bus drivers.
4 Money will be replaced by smart cards.
5 Television sets will also be computers.
6 Speech will be the main way of inputting data.
7 Computers will talk back to you.
8 Most shopping will be done using the Internet.
9 Videophones will replace existing phones.
10 Flat panel screens will replace monitors.

Computing words and abbreviations

Task 7   Put the words from the list into the correct box.

address	decode	HTML	binary	Delphi
control	execute	JavaScript	C++	hexadecimal
data	decimal	Visual Basic	Java	store

Computer languages	Buses	Number systems	Machine cycle

Task 8   Study these terms and their meanings.

an insect-sized robot   (a robot which is the size of an insect)
computer-generated graphics   (graphics which are generated by a computer)

Write the meaning of each of these terms.

1 an ant-sized machine
2 a head-mounted display
3 computer-assisted instruction
4 an IT-based future
5 computer-aided design
6 computer-aided manufacturing
7 character-based operating system
8 write-protected disk

Writing

Task 9   1 Describe some of the important developments in computing with the help of the information given in *Tuning-in*. Use the past passive in your description.

Example   *The transistor **was invented** in 1947.*
*The first generation of computers **were operated** by valves.*

2 Describe how developments in computing will affect homes in the future.

26 Issues in computing

Tuning-in

Task 1   Work in groups. Discuss how you can prevent these events.
1   Your files are accidentally destroyed.
2   Someone reads your private emails.
3   Someone copies software only you are authorized to use.

Task 2   How many ways can you think of for protecting a computer from unauthorized use? Note down your ideas and compare your list with another student.

Listening: Access systems

Task 3   Listen to this recording and make notes about each type of access system in the table.

Access system	Examples
What you have	
What you know	
Who you are	

Reading: Viruses

Task 4   Try to answer these questions in your group.
1   What is a computer virus?
2   How are viruses spread?
3   How can you deal with viruses?
4   Name any viruses you know.

Task 5   Read this text to check your answers to Task 4. Then find the answers to these questions.
1   List three computer crimes.
2   What do you think these words in the passage mean?
   flash (line 10)
   gobbledegook (line 15)
   dormant (line 19)
   eradicate (line 31)
3   Why is it difficult to remove all viruses?
4   Complete this table.

Virus	Effect
Yankee Doodle	
Cascade	
Michelangelo	
Jerusalem B	

Computer viruses

The Maltese Amoeba may sound like a cartoon character, but if it
attacked your computer, you wouldn't be laughing. The Maltese
Amoeba is a computer virus. It is a form of software which can
'infect' your system and destroy your data. Making computer
viruses is only one type of computer crime. Others include hacking   5
(changing data in a computer without permission) and pirating
(illegally copying software programs).

Viruses are programs which are written deliberately to damage data.
Viruses can hide themselves in a computer system. Some viruses
are fairly harmless. They may flash a message on screen, such as   10
'Gotcha! Bet you don't know how I crept in'. The Yankee Doodle virus
plays this American tune on the computer's small internal speaker
every eight days at 5 p.m. Others have serious effects. They attach
themselves to the operating system and can wipe out all your data
or turn it into gobbledegook. When the Cascade virus attacks, all   15
the letters in a file fall into a heap at the bottom of the screen. This
looks spectacular but it's hard to see the funny side when it's your
document.

Most viruses remain dormant until activated by something. For
example, the Jerusalem B virus is activated every Friday the 13th   20
and erases any file you try to load from your disk. The Michelangelo
virus was programmed to become active on March 6th 1992, the
517th birthday of Michelangelo. It attacked computer systems
throughout the world, turning data on hard disks into nonsense.

Viruses are most commonly passed via disks but they can also   25
spread through bulletin boards, local area networks, and email
attachments. The best form of treatment is prevention. Use an
antivirus program to check a disk before using it. Always
download email attachments onto a disk and check for viruses. If you
do catch a virus, there are antivirus programs to hunt down and   30
eradicate the virus. The problem is that around 150 new viruses
appear every month and you must constantly update your antivirus
package to deal with these new forms.

Language work: Making guidelines and rules

Study these guidelines for preventing and treating viruses.

Download email attachments onto a floppy.
Don't use a floppy without checking it.

We can make them stronger by adding *always* and *never*.

Always *download email attachments onto a floppy.*
Never *use a floppy without checking it.*

We can make them into rules by using using *must* and *mustn't*.

You **must** *download attachments onto a floppy.*
You **mustn't** *use a floppy without checking it.*

Task 6　Rewrite this advice using *must* or *mustn't*.

1　Keep your network password secret.
2　Don't try to access other people's data.
3　Always make a backup copy of all your important files.
4　Never use commercial software without a licence.
5　Check your email regularly.
6　Never install software before it is virus-checked.
7　Don't reuse Web images from pages which have a copyright symbol.
8　Never change other people's data without permission.
9　Don't believe every email message that warns you about viruses.
10　Always virus-check an email attachment before opening it.

Task 7　Write two rules about each of these topics.

1　passwords
2　floppy disk care
3　backups
4　working conditions
5　viruses
6　CD-ROM care

Problem-solving

Task 8 These headlines cover some of the ethical issues involved in computing. Work in pairs. Try to match the headlines to the first sentence of each story.

1   **NET BOMB BLAST INJURES BOYS**

2   **Cyberspace faces crucial court test**

3   **Police turning cybercop to net villains**

4   **Fears that new virus causes Internet chaos**

5   **CRIME AND PUNISHMENT**

a **The Internet may prove to be** a superhighway to crime for technologically-minded villains, the head of the National Criminal Intelligence Service has warned.

The Scotsman

b **An historic test case in a German court is to weigh the ethical and commercial question of who controls information on the Internet with the** American online services company CompuServe being accused of trafficking in pornography and neo-Nazi propaganda.

The Guardian

c The Federation Against Software Theft (FAST) and the mid-Glamorgan Trading Standards office have employed forensic technology to nab a software pirate.

PC Pro

d **Two 16-year-old Finnish schoolboys could face serious charges after a bomb they were making from** instructions found on the Internet blew up.

The Guardian

e **If you switch on your computer today and a sign appears saying 'You have GOT to read this' – do not** be tempted, because hidden in this email is a sinister new virus.

The Scotsman

Writing

Task 9 With the help of Task 2 and the recording, write guidelines and rules for protecting a computer from unauthorized use.

27 Careers in computing

Tuning-in

Task 1   Work in groups. List some of the jobs you know in computing. Compare your lists with other students in the class.

Task 2   Which of the jobs listed would you like to make your career? Explain why to others in your group.

Reading: Computing jobs

Task 3   Work in groups of three, A, B, and C. Read these descriptions of jobs in computing and make notes about the main responsibilities.

Group A   Read descriptions 1–2
Group B   Read descriptions 3–4
Group C   Read descriptions 5–6

Example

Systems Analyst

Studies methods of working within an organization to decide how tasks can be done efficiently by computers. Makes a detailed analysis of the employer's requirements and work patterns to prepare a report on different options for using information technology. This may involve consideration of hardware as well as software. Either uses standard computer packages or writes a specification for programmers to adapt existing software or to prepare new software. May oversee the implementation and testing of a system and acts as a link between the user and the programmer.

Job	Main responsibilities
Systems analyst	*Studies employer's requirements and working patterns. Reports on different options. Writes specifications for programmers. Oversees implementation and testing.*

1

Software Engineer/Designer

Produces the programs which control the internal operations of computers. Converts the system analyst's specification to a logical series of steps. Translates these into the appropriate computer language. Often compiles programs from libraries or sub-programs, combining these to make up a complete systems program. Designs, tests, and improves programs for computer-aided design and manufacture, business applications, computer networks, and games.

2 **Computer Salesperson**

Advises potential customers about available hardware and sells equipment to suit individual requirements. Discusses computing needs with the client to ensure that a suitable system can be supplied. Organizes the sale and delivery and, if necessary, installation and testing. May arrange support or training, maintenance, and consultation. Must have sufficient technical knowledge.

3 **Computer Systems Support Person**

Systems support people are analyst programmers who are responsible for maintaining, updating, and modifying the software used by a company. Some specialize in software which handles the basic operation of the computers. This involves the use of machine codes and specialized low-level computer languages. Most handle applications software. May sort out problems encountered by users. Solving problems may involve amending an area of code in the software, retrieving files and data lost when a system crashes, and a basic knowledge of hardware.

4 **Computer Systems Analyst Programmer**

Creates the software programs used by computers. May specialize in the internal operating systems using low level computer language, or in applications programs. May specialize in one aspect of the work, e.g. programming, systems design, systems analysis, or cover them all. May support the system through advice and training, providing user manuals, and by helping users with any problems that arise.

5 **Hardware Engineer**

Researches, designs, and develops computers, or parts of computers and the computerized element of appliances, machines, and vehicles. Also involved in their manufacture, installation, and testing. May specialize in different areas: research and development, design, manufacturing. Has to be aware of cost, efficiency, safety, and environmental factors, as well as engineering aspects.

6 **Network Support Person**

Maintains the link between PCs and workstations connected in a network. Uses telecommunications, software, and electronic skills, and knowledge of the networking software to locate and correct faults. This may involve work with the controlling software, on the wiring, printed circuit boards, software or microchips on a file server, or on cables either within or outside the building.

Task 4   Exchange information with other students in your group.

Listening: Talking about work

🔊 **Task 5** Listen to this recording of five people employed in computing talking about their work. Try to match each extract to the correct job from this list.

a ☐ Hardware Engineer   e ☐ Systems Analyst Programmer

b ☐ Network Support Person   f ☐ Systems Support Person

c ☐ Operator   g ☐ Technical Sales Manager

d ☐ Software Designer

Language work: Job requirements

Study some of the requirements for the job of Computer Network Support Person.

Essential

1 Diploma in computing or telecommunications engineering
2 Good communication skills to discuss requirements with users
3 Deductive ability for analysing faults
4 Able to work quickly under pressure
5 Normal colour vision to follow colour-coding of wires

Desirable

6 Interest in technology to keep up with new developments
7 Physically fit for lifting, carrying, and bending

We can describe the essential requirements like this.

*They **must have** a diploma in computing or telecommunications engineering.*
*They **must have** normal colour vision.*

We can describe the desirable requirements like this.

*They **should have** an interest in technology.*
*They **should be** physically fit.*

Task 6   Study these requirements for a Computer Technical Salesperson. Decide which are essential and which are desirable. Then describe each requirement using *must have/be* or *should have/be*.

1 a certificate or diploma in computing
2 experience in the computer industry
3 able to put technical ideas into everyday language
4 able to persuade and negotiate
5 a qualification in marketing
6 a thorough understanding of the product
7 a driving licence
8 a high level of communication skills
9 patient, persistent, and diplomatic
10 able to work away from home

Problem-solving

Task 7 Study this job advertisement. Which of the three candidates do you think is the best applicant?

IT Support Officer

■ Educated to degree level, candidates should have at least two years' relevant experience.

■ We need a highly-motivated individual, able to support approximately 30 networked PCs. The role is very much 'hands-on', and so it is essential that you have a good understanding and experience of Microsoft Office, Novell networks, Email systems, TCP/IP, hardware and virus-protection tools.

■ You should be able to communicate well with users and external contractors and to make a contribution to the training of all PC users.

■ The successful candidate must work well under pressure and as a team member.

Applicant 1

BSc Computing Science. Graduated this year.
- Knowledge of a variety of operating systems including Unix, Novell, and Windows XP
- Experience in programming in C, C++, Pascal, Java, Delphi and Visual Basic
- Familiar with a wide variety of hardware and software packages
- Has taught a lot of fellow students how to use computers
- Highly motivated
- No work experience

Applicant 2

Higher National Diploma in Information Technology
- Trained in using network systems including Novell and Windows XP
- Experienced user of Microsoft Office programs and Internet systems
- Knowledge of setting up and troubleshooting most types of computers and peripherals
- Gets on well with others and can work as part of a team
- Keen to gain experience and develop a career in computing
- Two years' part-time summer experience working in a computer repair workshop

Applicant 3

Higher National Certificate in Computing
- Employed for 3 years in a computing sales team advising customers on purchase requirements and helping them troubleshoot problems with installed systems
- Trained in using Unix and Novell network systems and a wide variety of hardware
- Experienced in many PC packages including most Microsoft products
- Good communicator, experienced in dealing with the public and working as part of a team
- Highly motivated

Writing

Task 8 Your teacher will give you an example of a CV. Write your own CV on the same model. If you are still a student, you may invent work experience for the purpose of this task.

28 Interview: Systems Manager

Tuning-in

Task 1 Study the job advertisement below and decide whether the statements (1–7) are true or false.

The successful applicant:

1 will develop new systems him/herself
2 must have at least five years' work experience
3 must have worked in a company
4 must be a good communicator
5 must know VB
6 must know SQL
7 will work alone.

Systems Manager	**Working closely with in-house users, you will be responsible for commissioning new systems and for maintaining and enhancing existing systems for a major retail company. You will be part of the management team.** • You will have a minimum of five years' experience in software development in a business environment. • You should have a good knowledge of VB and Access and have experience of Novell networks. Experience with Oracle and SQL would also be an advantage. • Good communication skills are essential and the ability to work as part of a team. **To find out more, email your CV to: steve.bell@pathfinder.com.uk**

Listening

Task 2 Bill is a Systems Manager with Britain's largest brewer. Listen to Part 1 of the interview and find the answers to these questions.

1 Which division of the company does Bill work for?

2 List his responsibilities.

3 Complete the missing steps in this procedure:

a Fault reported

b _____

c Fault investigated and fixed

d _____

e Details downloaded to a PC

f _____

g Activity recorded

h _____

i New parts ordered

4 Why does the company buy in systems?

5 What does Bill look for when buying a new system?

Listen to Part 2 and find the answers to these questions.

1 How many systems are there in the Beer Division?
2 What problem is there because old and new systems are running together?
3 List three ways in which the systems are protected.
4 What development is making a difference to the company?
5 What is Bill's view on the chance of a paper-free office in the future?

Language work: Revision

Task 4 Put the verbs in brackets into the correct tense.

1 Bill _____ (work) for the company for the last twenty-five years.
2 He _____ (graduate) in business studies and _____ (take) a job in London.
3 He _____ (train) as a systems analyst while he _____ (work) in London.
4 Now he _____ (look after) all the systems used by the Technical Services Division.
5 At the moment he _____ (develop) a system for handling repairs.
6 When something _____ (go) wrong in a pub, a service engineer _____ (send) to fix it.
7 Details of every repair _____ (download) to the company's mainframe each night.
8 No changes can _____ (make) until the system _____ (test).
9 Bill thinks that communications _____ (get) faster and faster in the future.
10 He thinks that a paper-free office _____ (not happen).

Task 5 Fill in the gaps with the correct form of an appropriate verb from this list.

may	might	must	should	will

1 Technicians _____ have normal colour vision to follow colour-coding of wires.
2 You _____ try to remove a floppy disk when the drive is running.
3 Biological computers _____ replace electronic computers in the future.
4 You _____ update your webpage regularly.
5 You _____ have pages with dead-ends on your website.
6 You _____ know your password to gain access to the network.
7 Computers _____ get cheaper and more powerful.
8 You _____ back up your files regularly.

Speaking

Task 6 Work in pairs, **A** and **B**. Your partner has one of the computing jobs listed in Unit 27. Find out about his/her occupation by asking questions like these.

Where do you work?   *How long have you been working there?*
What do you do?   *What qualifications do you have?*

Try to identify his/her occupation when you have asked these questions.

Student A Your job description is on page 118.
Student B Your job description is on page 119.

Problem-solving

Task 7 Study this diagram. It shows how face recognition can protect your computer system. Fill in the gaps in the text, using the information in the diagram and the words in the list.

Face recognition

Relatively expensive
Although the software alone is not expensive, you need to buy a video camera for every area you want to protect.

Unobtrusive
Face recognition requires no special action from the person using it.

Difficult setup
Video cameras make face recognition more difficult to set up than fingerprinting.

High accuracy
Face recognition is accurate, and the software provides an audit trail – with time, date, and face – of anyone trying to break into your PC.

Taxing
Full-motion video uses a lot of computing power.

accuracy	length	recognition	taxing	camera
recognize	database	features	unobtrusive	distance

Biometric security technology operates on the basis that we all have unique, measurable ¹_____, such as fingerprints. A computer system can
²_____ and verify these. There are two techniques used in face
³_____. The first compares the size and arrangement of facial
features – for example, the ⁴_____ of your nose and the
⁵_____ between your eyes. The other matches the most significant
feature of your face, such as your nose, with a ⁶_____ record.

116

The cost is quite high, as you need a [7]_____ for each computer. In addition, it is difficult to set up the camera to photograph all the features needed to make the procedure work. Video images are also [8]_____ on processing power. However, there is a high level of [9]_____. The system can still recognize you even if you change your hairstyle. In addition, the system is [10]_____. It photographs the face of the operator without any special action from them.

Computing words

Task 8a Match words from columns A and B to make common computing terms.

A	B
hardware	card
systems	board
file	recognition
swipe	wallet
voice	crime
computer	engineer
bulletin	server
electronic	analyst

Task 8b Which words in column B are commonly found with the verbs in column A?

A	B
analyse	data
browse	databases
debug	documents
delete	files
edit	folders
install	hardware
open	folders
run	needs
save	options
select	programs
	requirements
	software
	texts
	webpages
	websites

Student A Pair work

Unit 4

Task 10
1. ehg@ed.ac.uk
2. http://www.cltr.uq.oz.au
3. agoralang.com/agora/
   agoranews_current.html
4. http://www.ncl.ac.uk/~njw5
5. elvis@aol.com

Unit 7

Task 5

Screen size	21 inches
Aperture grill pitch	0.24 mm
Maximum resolution	1600×1200
Refresh rate	80 Hz
Price	£448

Unit 8

Task 11

Storage device	Capacity
DVD	4.7 - 18.8GB
High density floppy	1.44MB
Hard disk	20Gb
CD-ROM	
Large hard disk	
Tape	

Unit 12

Task 10
1. Make your letters big
2. Use simple shapes
3. Use block printing

> EWING
> 57320
> KENT

Unit 16

Task 11

new   print   copy

drawing

Unit 20

Task 10   Program A

```
10//  Logic error 1
20    FOR times: = 2 to 10
30    IF times = 1 THEN PRINT
      "HELLO"
40    NEXT times
50    END
```

Unit 22

Task 12   Change 1011 binary to decimal.

Step 1
   place values 8 4 2 1
   binary   1 0 1 1

Step 2
   $(1\times8)+(0\times4)+(1\times2)+(1\times1) =11$

Start like this: *Write down the place values: 8, 4, 2 and 1. These are powers of 2.*

Unit 24

Task 12

Biometrics – eye scanning
1. Person arrives at airport scanner
2. Person looks through eyepiece
3. Laser scans eye and records microscopic details
4. Computer translates data into unique barcode
5. Computer checks digital image against central database
6. Person's identity confirmed

Unit 28

Task 6

Systems Analyst
You work in a large hospital. You collect and analyse information about hospital procedures. You get the information by talking to the doctors, nurses, and administrators in the hospital. You identify tasks that computers can do so that time and money can be saved. Then you design a system to perform these tasks.

You've been working in this job for five years. You've also worked for a software company. You have a degree in business studies but you later trained as a systems analyst.

Student B Pair work

Unit 4

Task 10
1 jtp@gl.ac.uk
2 http://calico.org/
3 http://info.ox.ac.uk
4 http://www.dart.edu/~hr/lrc/
5 bluff.t@ozemail.com.au

Unit 7

Task 5

Screen size	17 inches
Aperture grill pitch	0.26 mm
Maximum resolution	1280×1024
Refresh rate	75 Hz
Price	£319

Unit 8

Task 11

Storage device	Capacity
DVD	
High density floppy	
Hard disk	
CD-ROM	650MB
Large hard disk	100GB
Tape	8GB

Unit 12

Task 10
4 Connect lines
5 Close loops
6 Do not link characters

```
5BE4
9068
LOOP
```

Unit 16

Task 11

save   cut

undo   insert table

Unit 20

Task 10 Program B
```
10// Logic error 2
20    total: = 0
30    REPEAT
40    total: = total + 1
50    UNTIL total = 0
60    END
```

Unit 22

Task 12 Change 27 decimal to binary.

```
2/27
2/13  R1
2/ 6  R1
2/ 3  R0
   1  R1
```
Binary = 11011

Start like this: *Divide the number by two and write down the remainder (R).*

Unit 24

Task 12 Biometrics – hand scanning
1 Person arrives at airport scanner
2 Person inserts credit card into console
3 Person inserts hand to be scanned
4 Computer checks handprint against central database
5 Computer checks handprint matches credit card details
6 Person's identity confirmed

Unit 28

Task 6 **Computer Services Engineering Technician**

You work for a computer service firm. You repair computers and other devices such as printers. You also upgrade computers. People phone in when they have a problem and you go to their company, find out what is wrong, and repair the fault.

This is your first job. You've been working for the firm for two years. You have a diploma in Computer Systems Engineering.

Glossary
of computing terms and abbreviations

A

active badge /ˌæktɪv ˈbædʒ/ *n* C [26] a smartcard device worn by the user

Active Server page /ˌæktɪv ˈsɜːvə ˌpeɪdʒ/ *n* C [20] a type of webpage that contains a script that is processed on a web server

active window /ˈæktɪv ˌwɪndəʊ/ *n* C [9] the window in a WIMP system that is currently being used. It is usually on top of any other open windows.

add-on /ˈæd ˌɒn/ *n* C [15] a small program that can be attached to a browser program to give the browser extra functions

address box /əˈdres ˌbɒks/ *n* C [14] the area in a web browser program where the web address is displayed

address bus /əˈdres ˌbʌs/ *n* C [22] the set of conductors that carry the memory address signals between different parts of a computer system

ALU /ˌeɪ el ˈjuː/ *n* C [22] abbreviation for arithmetic and logic unit

amend /əˈmend/ *v* [27] to make corrections

analogue signal /ˈænəlɒg ˌsɪgnəl/ *n* C [12] a type of signal that can take any value between a maximum and a minimum

analogue-to-digital converter /ˌænəlɒg tə ˌdɪdʒɪtl kənˈvɜːtə(r)/ *n* C [6] a device for changing analogue signals into digital signals

animation /ˌænɪˈmeɪʃn/ *n* C [2,15] drawings that have moving images

anti-virus program /ˌænti ˈvaɪrəs ˌprəʊgræm/ *n* C [26] a set of programs used to detect, identify, and remove viruses from a system

aperture grill pitch /ˌæpətʃə ˌgrɪl ˈpɪtʃ/ *n* C [7] the distance between the holes or slots in the filter screen inside a monitor

Apple Macintosh /ˌæpl ˈmækɪntɒʃ/ *n* C [25] a type of personal computer manufactured by Apple Computer Incorporated

application /ˌæplɪˈkeɪʃn/ *n* C [10] See **applications program**.

applications (program or software) /ˌæplɪˈkeɪʃnz/ *n* C, U [27] a computer program or programs designed to be used for a particular purpose

arithmetic and logic unit /əˌrɪθmətɪk ənd ˈlɒdʒɪk ˌjuːnɪt/ *n* C [22] the part of the CPU that performs the mathematical and logical operations

arrow keys /ˈærəʊ ˌkiːz/ *n* Pl [4] the set of four keys on a keyboard used for moving the cursor around the screen

assembly language /əˈsembli ˌlæŋgwɪdʒ/ *n* C [21] a low-level computer language that uses mnemonics rather than only numbers, making it easier than machine code for humans to read and write

B

back up /ˌbæk ˈʌp/ *v* [8] to store a copy of data on a storage device to keep it safe

backup /ˈbækʌp/ *n* C [8] the process of storing a copy of data on a storage device to keep it safe

backup device /ˈbækʌp dɪˌvaɪs/ *n* C [11] a storage device used for copying files to a storage medium to keep them safe

barcode /ˈbɑːkəʊd/ *n, v* C [1] a sequence of vertical parallel lines used to give items a unique identification number / to mark with a barcode

barcode label /ˈbɑːkəʊd ˌleɪbl/ *n* C [1] a label that is used to attach a barcode to an item

barcode reader /ˈbɑːkəʊd ˌriːdə(r)/ *n* C [1] an optical input device that uses the reflection of a light beam to read barcode labels

batch job /ˈbætʃ ˌdʒɒb/ *n* C [28] sets of data to be processed together by a mainframe computer

bidirectional /ˌbaɪdɪ-, ˌbaɪdaɪ- ˈrekʃənl/ *adj* [22] designed to carry signals in either direction

binary /ˈbaɪnəri/ *adj* [6, 22] belonging to the number system that has only two digits, i.e. 1 and 0

bit /bɪt/ *n* C [8] a small unit of storage capacity / one of the eight binary digits that make up a byte. The term comes from an abbreviation of binary digit.

bookmark /ˈbʊkmɑːk/ *n, v* [15] a web address stored in a browser program to allow a webpage to be found easily / to store a web address in a browser program to allow a webpage to be found easily

branch /brɑːntʃ/ *n* C [19] a point in a program or flowchart where there are two possible paths

browser /ˈbraʊzə(r)/ *n* C [14] a program used for displaying webpages

bulletin board /ˈbʊlətɪn ˌbɔːd/ *n* C [26] a kind of electronic noticeboard system that enables users to display messages for other users to read

bus /bʌs/ *n* C [22] the set of conductors that carry the signals between different parts of a computer

bus topology /ˌbʌs təˈpɒlədʒi/ *n* C [11] a physical layout of a network where all the computers are attached to one main cable terminated at both ends

byte /baɪt/ *n* C [3] a unit of capacity. A byte is made up of eight bits and stores one character, i.e. a letter, a number, a space or a punctuation mark.

C

cache memory /ˈkæʃ ˌmeməri/ *n* U [3] high speed memory used to speed up a computer

CCD /ˌsiː siː ˈdiː/ *n* C [6] abbreviation for charge-coupled device

CD-ROM (disk) /ˌsiː diː ˈrɒm/ *n* C [2, 8] abbreviation for compact disk read-only memory. A read-only storage device (a disk) that is read using laser light.

CD-ROM drive /ˌsiː diː ˈrɒm ˌdraɪv/ n C [2, 8] a storage device for reading CD-ROM disks

cell /sel/ n C [17] the rectangular box formed where a row and a column meet in a spreadsheet

central processing unit /ˌsentrəl ˈprəʊsesɪŋ ˌjuːnɪt/ n C [22] the electronic processor at the centre of a computer. It is sometimes used to refer to the combination of the processor and the main memory.

charge-coupled device /ˈtʃɑːdʒ ˌkʌpld dɪˌvaɪs/ n C [6] an electronic semiconductor camera device

checkbox /ˈtʃekbɒks/ n C [9] a dialog box component in the form of a small square box used to indicate one of two alternative states, e.g. true or false. When the user clicks the box with a mouse, a cross appears in the box. Clicking again clears the box.

chip /tʃɪp/ n C [3] common name for a microchip

click /klɪk/ v [3, 9] to press and release a button on a mouse

client /ˈklaɪənt/ n C [11] a network computer used for accessing a service on a server

clock chip /ˈklɒk ˌtʃɪp/ n C [22] the electronic device in a computer that controls the timing of the signals

clock line /ˈklɒk ˌlaɪn/ n C [22] the conductor that carries the clock signal to different parts of the computer

coax(ial) cable /ˈkəʊæks, kəʊˈæksiəl ˌkeɪbl/ n C [12] a type of shielded cable for carrying signals. It is often used with radio frequency and video signals.

code /kəʊd/ n, v U [19, 20] a program written in a computer language / to write a program using a computer language

COM port /ˈkɒm ˌpɔːt/ n C [3] another name for a serial port (from an abbreviation for communications)

command button /kəˈmɑːnd ˌbʌtn/ n C [14] a dialog box component that takes the form of a rectangular icon that causes a program command to be carried out when clicked with a mouse

communications link /kəˌmjuːnɪˈkeɪʃnz ˌlɪŋk/ n C [12] a connection between two points for transmitting and receiving signals

compilation error /ˌkɒmpɪˈleɪʃn ˌerə(r)/ n C [20] a programming error that prevents a program from being converted into machine code by a compiler

compile /kəmˈpaɪl/ v [27] to convert a program written in a high-level language into machine code using a compiler

compiler /kəmˈpaɪlə(r)/ n C [19] a program that converts the whole of a program into machine code before the program is used

computer aided design /kəmˌpjuːtə ˌeɪdɪd dɪˈzaɪn/ n C [27] the process of designing using a computer program

computing /kəmˈpjuːtɪŋ/ n U [5] the theory and practice of computers

control bus /kənˈtrəʊl ˌbʌs/ n C [22] the set of conductors that carry the control signals between the control unit and other parts of a computer

control unit /kənˈtrəʊl ˌjuːnɪt/ n C [22] the part of the CPU that generates the signals that control the computer programs and hardware

copyholder /ˈkɒpɪˌhəʊldə(r)/ n C [7] a mechanical device for holding a piece of paper when it is being read

CPU /ˌsiː piː ˈjuː/ n C [22] abbreviation for central processing unit

crash /kræʃ/ n, v C [8] a sudden and complete failure / to fail suddenly and completely

Cray /kreɪ/ n C [25] a well-known make of very powerful supercomputer

CU /ˌsiː ˈjuː/ n C [22] abbreviation for control unit

cursor /ˈkɜːsə(r)/ n C [4, 9] the symbol on the monitor screen that indicates the point on the screen that is being used

cursor keys /ˈkɜːsə ˌkiːz/ n Pl [4] See **arrow keys**.

data /ˈdeɪtə/ n U [4] the information processed by a computer

data bus /ˈdeɪtə ˌbʌs/ n C [22] the set of conductors that carry the data signals between different parts of a computer

data processing department /ˌdeɪtə ˈprəʊsesɪŋ dɪˌpɑːtmənt/ n C [28] a department of computing professionals where data is processed in batches on a mainframe computer

database /ˈdeɪtəbeɪs/ n C [5,17] a type of application program used for storing information so that it can be easily searched and sorted

dataglove /ˈdeɪtəglʌv/ n C [23] an input device worn on the hand in a virtual reality system

debug /ˌdiːˈbʌg/ v [19] to find and fix the faults in a program or system

decimal /ˈdesɪml/ adj [22] belonging to the number system that has ten digits: 0, 1, 2, 3, 4, 5, 6, 7, 8, 9

decode /ˌdiːˈkəʊd/ v [22] to decide what a program instruction means

desktop (computer) /ˈdesktɒp (kəmˈpjuːtə)/ n C [2] a personal computer designed to sit on a desk

desktop publishing package /ˌdesktɒp ˈpʌblɪʃɪŋ ˌpækɪdʒ/ n C [18] an application program that is used for creating and editing the text and layout of pages to be published

dialog box /ˈdaɪəlɒg ˌbɒks/ n C [9] a window in a WIMP system that is used to provide information or obtain information from the user

digital camera /ˌdɪdʒɪtl ˈkæmərə/ n C [6] an input device for taking pictures that has an electronic lens and uses electronics for storing the images rather than chemical film

digital signal /ˌdɪdʒɪtl ˈsɪgnl/ n C [12] a signal that only has one of two values representing on or off

direct neural interface /ˌdaɪrekt, dɪˌrekt ˌnjʊərəl ˈɪntəfeɪs/ n C [23] a device that enables electronic signals to be input to and output from the human brain

disk /dɪsk/ n C [1, 8] a flat circular storage device

disk drive /ˈdɪsk ˌdraɪv/ n C [3, 8] a storage device for reading from and writing to disks

distributed computing /dɪˌstrɪbjutɪd kəmˈpjuːtɪŋ/ n U [25] a network system that uses different servers throughout the network rather than a single server at the centre of the network

DNI /ˌdiː en ˈaɪ/ n C [23] an abbreviation for direct neural interface

dot pitch /ˌdɒt ˈpɪtʃ/ n C [7] the distance between the dots on a monitor screen

121

dot-matrix printer /ˌdɒt ˈmeɪtrɪks ˌprɪntə(r)/ *n* C [7] a printer that prints by hammering pins onto an inked ribbon

double density floppy (disk) /ˌdʌbl ˌdensəti ˈflɒpi/ *n* C [8] a removable magnetic storage device in the form of a plastic disk that can hold about 712 kilobytes of data

download /ˈdaʊnləʊd/ *v* [6,14] to copy a file from a server to a client computer in a network

drag /dræg/ *v* [18] to move an object across the display screen by moving a mouse while holding down the mouse button

drop-down list box /ˌdrɒpdaʊn ˈlɪst ˌbɒks/ *n* C [9] a dialog box component that opens a list of items when the user clicks on the arrowhead at the end

drop-down menu /ˌdrɒpdaʊn ˈmenju:/ *n* C [16] a list of options that opens downwards and stays open when clicked with a mouse

dry run /ˌdraɪ ˈrʌn/ *n* C [19] a test of a program by checking through it on paper before running it on a computer

DVD /ˌdi: ˌvi: ˈdi:/ *n* C [3] abbreviation for digital versatile disk. An optical disk storage device that can hold a large amount of video data

dye sublimation printer /ˈdaɪ ˌsʌblɪmˌeɪʃn ˈprɪntə/ *n* C [7] a type of colour printer that prints by heating dye that is transferred onto special paper.

E-time /ˈi:taɪm/ *n* C [22] a common name for the execution time

earth satellite station /ˌ3:θ ˈsætəlaɪt ˌsteɪʃn/ *n* C [12] an installation on Earth used for sending and receiving signals to and from a satellite

earth-satellite transmission /ˌ3:θ ˌsætəlaɪt trænsˈmɪʃn/ *n* C [12] the process of sending a signal to, or receiving a signal from, a satellite orbiting the Earth

edit /ˈedɪt/ *v* [16] to make changes to

editing keys /ˈedɪtɪŋ ˌki:z/ *n* Pl [4] the set of keys on a PC keyboard to the right of the main keyboard that is used for moving around the screen and making changes to a document

electronic wallet /ˌelektrɒnɪk ˈwɒlɪt/ *n* C [24] a smartcard used for storing money downloaded from a computer bank account

email /ˈi:meɪl/ *n, v* U [1,4,13] the common name for electronic mail, i.e. messages sent electronically using a computer / to send an email message

email address /ˈi:meɪl əˌdres/ *n* C [4,6,13] the unique address code used to contact someone using electronic mail

email attachment /ˈi:meɪl əˌtætʃmənt/ *n* C [13] a file that is attached to an email message

embed /emˈbed/ *v* [21] to insert an object inside another object

encode /enˈkəʊd/ *v* [23] to write information in a coded form

execute /ˈeksɪkju:t/ *v* [22] to perform a computer operation by processing a program instruction

execution time /eksɪˈkju:ʃn ˌtaɪm/ *n* C [22] the time taken to execute a program instruction and store the result in memory

expansion card /ɪkˈspænʃn ˌka:d/ *n* C [3] an electronic circuit board used for adding facilities to a computer

expansion slot /ɪkˈspænʃn ˌslɒt/ *n* C [3] a long thin connector that is used for adding additional electronics in the form of expansion cards

export /ekˈspɔ:t/ *v* [6] to bring data out of a program in a form suitable for use by another program

extended keyboard /ɪkˌstendɪd ˈki:bɔ:d/ *n* C [4] the common arrangement of keys on a PC keyboard with editing keys and a numeric keypad to the right of the main keyboard

Far End /ˈfa:r ˌend/ *n* C [12] the equipment at the remote end of a video conferencing system

fetch /fetʃ/ *v* [22] to go and get the next instruction or piece of data from memory

fibre-optic(s) cable /ˌfaɪbər ˈɒptɪk(s) ˌkeɪbl/ *n* C [12] a cable made from strands of glass that is used for carrying information signals on a beam of light

field /fi:ld/ *n* C [17] a section of a database where an item of data is stored

file /faɪl/ *n* C [8] a computer program or data stored on a storage device

file server /ˈfaɪl ˌsɜ:və(r)/ *n* C [27] a main computer that provides a data file store on a network

flicker-free /ˈflɪkəfri:/ *adj* [7] having no variation in the brightness of the display of a monitor screen

floppy (disk) /ˈflɒpi/ *n* C [3,8] a magnetic storage device in the form of a small plastic disk (also known as a diskette)

floppy (disk) drive /ˈflɒpi ˌdraɪv/ *n* C [3,8] a common magnetic storage device that reads and writes data on a floppy disk

flowchart /ˈfləʊtʃa:t/ *n* C [7] a kind of diagram used by programmers to show the logical steps in a program

folder /ˈfəʊldə(r)/ *n* C [9] a way of grouping filenames so that the files can be easily located on a storage device. A folder is sometimes called a directory.

font /fɒnt/ *n* C [16] a set of text characters of a particular design

format (1) /ˈfɔ:mæt/ *n, v* C [16] the design and appearance of text in a document / to design the look of text in a document

format (2) /ˈfɔ:mæt/ *n, v* C [19] the arrangement of storage areas on a storage medium / to create storage areas on a storage medium

formatting toolbar /ˈfɔ:ˌmætɪŋ ˌtu:lba:(r)/ *n* C [16] a row of icons in a program, used to change the appearance of the text when clicked with a mouse

freeze /fri:z/ *v* [10] suddenly to stop responding. It is usually used in reference to a screen display.

function keys /ˈfʌŋkʃn ˌki:z/ *n* Pl [4] keyboard keys that are normally programmed to perform different functions by each program or by the user

GB /ˈgɪgəbaɪt/ *n* C [3,8] abbreviation for a gigabyte

general purpose package /ˌʤenrəl ˈpɜ:pəs ˌpækɪʤ/ *n* C [16] an application program that can be used in a variety of ways

giga /'gɪgə/ *prefix* [8] the prefix used for 10^9 in decimal or 2^{30} in binary

gigabyte /'gɪgəbaɪt/ *n C* [3] a capacity of 2^{30} bytes, i.e. 1024 megabytes

grandfather, father, son method, (the) /ˌgrænfɑːðə ˌfɑːðə ˈsʌn ˌmeθəd/ *n U* [14] a system for backing up files that uses three sets of backup media that are used in rotation

graphic /'græfɪk/ *n C* [1,18] a picture, drawing, animation or other type of image

graphical user interface /ˌgræfɪkl ˌjuːzər ˈɪntəfeɪs/ *n C* [9] part of an operating system that allows the user to interact with a computer using images and a cursor

graphics card /'græfɪks ˌkɑːd/ *n C* [3] an expansion board containing electronics for controlling the computer output to a monitor

graphics package /'græfɪks ˌpækɪʤ/ *n C* [14] a type of applications program that is used for creating and editing images and drawings

graphics tablet /'græfɪks ˌtæblət/ *n C* [6] a graphical input device that tracks the movement of a stylus across a flat surface

GUI /'guːiː/ *n C* [9] abbreviation for graphical user interface

hacking /'hækɪŋ/ *n U* [26] the practice of breaking into computer systems and changing data without permission

handheld /'hændheld/ *n C* [2] a small portable computer that can be held in one hand. See **palmtop**.

hang /hæŋ/ *v* [10] suddenly and unexpectedly to stop processing during the execution of a program

hard (disk) (drive) /'hɑːd ˌdraɪv/ *n C* [3, 8] a common magnetic storage device that reads and writes data on metal disks inside a sealed case

hardware /'hɑːdweə(r)/ *n U* [2] the physical components of a computer system

high density floppy (disk) /ˌhaɪ ˌdensəti ˈflɒpi/ *n C* [8] a removable magnetic storage device in the form of a plastic disk that can hold about 1.4 megabytes of data, i.e. twice as much as a double density disk

high-level language /ˌhaɪ ˌlevl ˈlæŋgwɪʤ/ *n C* [19] a programming language closer to human language than low-level computer languages such as machine code or assembly language

home page /'həʊm ˌpeɪʤ/ *n C* [15] the starting page on a website

HTML /ˌeɪtʃtiːemˈel/ *n U* [20, 21] abbreviation for hypertext markup language / a computer language that uses a system of tags for creating web pages

hub /hʌb/ *n C* [11] an electronic device at the centre of a star network topology

Hz /hɜːts/ *n C* [7] abbreviation for hertz / the basic unit of frequency equal to one cycle per second

I-time /'aɪtaɪm/ *n C* [22] a common name for the instruction time

I.T. /ˌaɪ ˈtiː/ *n U* [5] abbreviation for information technology

IBM /ˌaɪbiːˈem/ *n U* [25] abbreviation for the computer company called International Business Machines Corporation

icon /'aɪkɒn/ *n C* [9] a small picture used in a WIMP system to represent a program, folder or file

information technology /ɪnfəˌmeɪʃn tekˈnɒləʤi/ *n U* [5] the study and practice of techniques or use of equipment for dealing with information

inkjet printer /'ɪŋkʤet ˌprɪntə(r)/ *n C* [7] a printer that prints by spraying ink onto paper

input /'ɪnpʊt/ *n, v C* [4, 6] data put into a system / to put data into a system

input device /'ɪnpʊt dɪˌvaɪs/ *n C* [6] a piece of equipment used for entering data or controlling a computer

insertion point /ɪnˈsɜːʃn ˌpɔɪnt/ *n C* [16] the position where something is put into a file

instruction /ɪnˈstrʌkʃn/ *n C* [22] one line of a computer program

instruction time /ɪnˈstrʌkʃn ˌtaɪm/ *n C* [22] the time taken to fetch and decode a program instruction

interface /'ɪntəfeɪs/ *n, v C* [9] the connection between two different systems / to provide a connection between two different systems

Internet service provider /ˌɪntənet ˈsɜːvɪs prəˌvaɪdə(r)/ *n C* [13] an organization that provides Internet connections for a fee

Internet, (the) /'ɪntənet/ *n U* [1,13,14] the connection of computer networks across the world

interpreter /ɪnˈtɜːprɪtə(r)/ *n C* [19] a program that converts other programs into machine code line by line as the programs are being used

interrupt /'ɪntərʌpt/ *n C* [22] a signal that causes the processor to stop what it is doing temporarily so that it can process something that is more urgent

ISP /ˌaɪesˈpiː/ *n C* [13] abbreviation for Internet service provider

jam /ʤæm/ *v* [10] to get stuck in one position

joystick /'ʤɔɪstɪk/ *n C* [6] a cursor control input device with an upright arm. It is commonly used for controlling fast moving objects in computer games.

justify /'ʤʌstɪfaɪ/ *v* [16] to insert spaces so that lines of a text are aligned on both the left and right sides at the same time

KB /'kɪləbaɪt/ *n C* [3] abbreviation for a kilobyte

keyboard /'kiːbɔːd/ *n C* [3, 4] the main electronic input device that has keys arranged in a similar layout to a typewriter

keypad /'kiːpæd/ *n C* [4] a small keyboard with a few keys used for a special purpose

kilo /'kiːləʊ/ *prefix* [3] the prefix used for 10^3 in decimal or 2^{10} in binary

kilobyte /'kɪləbaɪt/ *n C* [3] a capacity of 2^{10} bytes, i.e. 1024 bytes

LAN /læn/ *n* C [11] acronym for local area network

laptop (computer) /'læptɒp/ *n* C [2] the largest type of portable computer

laser /'leɪzə(r)/ *n* C [1] high frequency light used in optical devices

laser printer /'leɪzə ˌprɪntə(r)/ *n* C [7] a printer that prints using toner powder and laser light on a photosensitive drum

LCD /ˌelsiː'diː/ *n* C [6] abbreviation for liquid crystal display / an electronic display device that uses liquid crystal cells to control the reflection of light

library /'laɪbrəri/ *n* C [20] a set of programmed functions that are made available for use by any program

lightpen /'laɪtpen/ *n* C [6] a pen-shaped input device used for drawing on a display screen. It detects light on the screen.

linking error /'lɪŋkɪŋ ˌerə(r)/ *n* C [20] a programming mistake caused by trying to use a function from a program library that is not available

local area network /ˌləʊkl ˌeəriə 'netwɜːk/ *n* C [11] computers connected together over a small distance

log /lɒg/ *v* [28] to record the time that an event happened

logic error /'lɒdʒɪk ˌerə(r)/ *n* C [19] a programming mistake caused by the use of a sequence of instructions that are not logical

loop /luːp/ *n* C [20] a part of a program that is repeated until a set condition occurs

loudspeaker /ˌlaʊd'spiːkə(r)/ *n* C [3] a sound output device

low-level language /ˌləʊ ˌlevl 'læŋgwɪdʒ/ *n* C [21] a computer language such as machine code or assembly language that is closer to the form that a computer understands than to that of a human language

machine code /mə'ʃiːn ˌkəʊd/ *n* C [21] a computer language that consists entirely of a combination of 1s and 0s

machine cycle / mə'ʃiːn ˌsaɪkl/ *n* C [22] the complete processes performed by the CPU of fetching, decoding, executing, and storing the result of a program instruction

magnetic tape /mæg,netɪk 'teɪp/ *n* C [8] a magnetic storage medium in the form of a thin plastic ribbon wound on a reel or a cassette. It is commonly used for backing up data.

magneto-optical disk /mæg,netəʊ ˌɒptɪkl 'dɪsk/ *n* C [8] a storage device that uses a combination of magnetism and laser light to store data

main memory /ˌmeɪn 'meməri/ *n* U [22] the electronic memory that holds the programs and data being used

mainframe (computer) /'meɪnfreɪm/ *n* C [2] the largest and most powerful type of computer. It is operated by a team of professionals.

MB /'megəbaɪt/ *n* C [3] abbreviation for a megabyte

Medicard /'medɪkɑːd/ *n* C [23] a smartcard that stores medical information

mega /'megə/ *prefix* [3] the prefix used for 10^6 in decimal or 2^{20} in binary

megabyte /'megəbaɪt/ *n* C [3] a unit of capacity equal to 2^{20} bytes, i.e. 1024 kilobytes

megahertz /'megəhɜːts/ *n* C [3] a unit of frequency equal to 1 million cycles per second

megawatt /'megəwɒt/ *n* C [25] a unit of power equal to 1 million watts

memory (store) /'meməri/ *n* U [3] the part of a computer system that is used for storing programs and data

memory address /'meməri əˌdres/ *n* C [22] a code indicating the location of a unit of memory

memory chip /'meməri ˌtʃɪp/ *n* C [3] an electronic integrated circuit that is used for storing programs and data while they are being used by a computer

memory slot /'meməri ˌslɒt/ *n* C [3] a connector on the motherboard of a computer that enables extra memory chips to be added

menu /'menjuː/ *n* C [3, 6, 9] a list of options displayed on a computer screen

menu bar /'menjuː ˌbɑː(r)/ *n* C [14] a row of icons on a display screen that open up menus when selected

mesh topology /'meʃ təˌpɒlədʒi/ *n* C [11] an arrangement of computers in a network where every computer is connected to every other computer by a separate cable

MHz /'megəhɜːts/ *n* C [3] abbreviation for megahertz

micro-machine /'maɪkrəʊ məˌʃiːn/ *n* C [23] an extremely small mechanical mechanism that contains a tiny computer

microchip /'maɪkrəʊ ˌtʃɪp/ *n* C [27] an electronic integrated circuit in a small package

microcomputer /'maɪkrəʊkəmˌpjuːtə(r)/ *n* C [2] a personal computer, smaller and less powerful than a mainframe or a minicomputer

microlaser scanner glasses /ˌmaɪkrəʊleɪzə 'skænə ˌglɑːsɪz/ *n* Pl [23] Eye glasses used in virtual reality systems. They use a small laser device to project computer-generated images directly into the user's eye.

microphone /'maɪkrəfəʊn/ *n* C [6] an input device used for sound

microprocessor /ˌmaɪkrəʊ'prəʊsesə(r)/ *n* C [3] the main electronic chip in a computer. It can be thought of as the 'brain' of the computer because it does the main processing and controls the other parts of the computer. It is sometimes called the CPU.

microwave station /'maɪkrəweɪv ˌsteɪʃn/ *n* C [12] an installation for receiving and transmitting microwave signals

microwave transmission /ˌmaɪkrəweɪv træns'mɪʃn/ *n* C [12] the process of sending a high frequency signal known as a microwave

minicomputer /'mɪnɪkəmˌpjuːtə(r)/ *n* C [2] a computer that is slightly less powerful and a little smaller than a mainframe

modem /'məʊdem/ *n* C [2] an electronic device for converting signals to enable a computer to be connected to an ordinary telephone line. The term comes from an abbreviation of MODulator/ DEModulator.

monitor /'mɒnɪtə(r)/ *n* C [2] the main output device used to display the output from a computer on a screen. See **VDU**.

motherboard /'mʌðəbɔːd/ n C [3] the main electronic circuit board inside a computer that holds and connects together all the main electronic components

mouse /maʊs/ n C [3, 9] a common cursor control input device used with a graphical user interface. It has two or three button switches on top and a ball underneath that is rolled on a flat surface.

mouse button /'maʊs ˌbʌtn/ n C [4] a switch on a mouse that is pressed to select an object on the screen

mousemat /'maʊsmæt/ n C [4] the small pad that a mouse sits on

MPR-II /ˌempiːɑː ˈtuː/ n U [7] guidelines produced by the Swedish National Board for Measurement and Testing giving information on the measurement of emissions from visual display screens

MSDOS /ˌemesˈdɒs/ n U [5] trademark, abbreviation for Microsoft disk operating system / the operating system that was used in the first PCs

multimedia /ˌmʌltɪˈmiːdiə/ n U [2,18] the combination of text, graphics, animation, sound, and video

multimedia computer /ˌmʌltɪˈmiːdiə kəmˈpjuːtə(r)/ n C [2] a computer suitable for running multimedia programs. It usually has a sound card and a CD-ROM drive.

multiuser /ˌmʌltɪˈjuːzə(r)/ adj [2,13] capable of being used by many people at the same time

N

Near End /'nɪər ˌend/ n C [12] the equipment at the closest end of a video conferencing system

Net, (the) /net/ n U [20] the common name for the Internet

network /'netwɜːk/ n, v C [5,11] a combination of a number of computers and peripheral devices connected together / to connect a number of computers and peripheral devices together

network (interface) card /'netwɜːk ˌkɑːd/ n C [5] the electronic circuit board inside a computer that is used to connect the computer to a network

newsgroup /'njuːzgruːp/ n C [13] an Internet discussion group made up of people with a common interest who use an area on a server computer to display messages about their interest

notebook (computer) /'nəʊtbʊk/ n C [2] a portable computer that is about the same size as a piece of writing paper

O

OCR /ˌəʊsiːˈɑː(r)/ n U [6] abbreviation for optical character recognition

online /ˌɒnˈlaɪn/ adj, preposition [14] connected to a system and able to be used

operating system /'ɒpəreɪtɪŋ ˌsɪstəm/ n C [4] the set of programs that control the basic functions of a computer

optical character recognition /ˌɒptɪkl ˌkærɪktə ˌrekəgˈnɪʃn/ n U [6] a process that enables a computer to scan and recognize printed characters using the reflection of light

optical disk /ˌɒptɪkl ˈdɪsk/ n C [8, 22] a storage device in the form of a disk that uses laser light to store data

output /'aʊtpʊt/ n, v C [7] data brought out of a system / to bring data out of a system

output device /'aʊtpʊt dɪˌvaɪs/ n C [7] a piece of equipment used to bring data out of a system

P-I-P /ˌpiːaɪˈpiː/ adj [12] abbreviation for picture-in-picture

package /'pækɪdʒ/ n C [5] an application program or collection of programs that can be used in different ways

page-makeup program /ˌpeɪdʒ ˈmeɪkʌp ˌprəʊgræm/ n C [18] a program for designing the layout of a page for publishing

palmtop (computer) /'pɑːmtɒp/ n C [2] a portable computer that is small enough to be held in the palm of one hand. See **handheld**.

paper tape /ˌpeɪpə ˈteɪp/ n U [25] an obsolete computer input medium consisting of a ribbon of paper with holes punched in it

parallel port /'pærəlel ˌpɔːt/ n C [3] a long connector at the back of the system unit of a PC that is often used to connect a printer to the CPU

password /'pɑːswɜːd/ n C [9] a secret code used to control access to a network system

paste /peɪst/ v [18] to insert a copy of data held in the computer's memory at a chosen position

PC /ˌpiː ˈsiː/ n C [1, 2] abbreviation for an IBM type of personal computer, although sometimes used for other types of personal computer

PDA /ˌpiː diː ˈeɪ/ n C [2] abbreviation for personal digital assistant. A small handheld computer providing a variety of tools for organizing work, e.g. a calendar, to do list, diary, address list, calculator, etc.

peripheral /pəˈrɪfərəl/ n C [11] a piece of equipment that is connected to the central processing unit of a computer system

personal computer /ˌpɜːsənl kəmˈpjuːtə(r)/ n C [2] a computer designed to be used by one person at a time

picture-in-picture /ˌpɪktʃər ɪn ˈpɪktʃə(r)/ adj [12] a display screen feature that has a video picture displayed inside another video picture

PIN /pɪn/ n C [24] abbreviation for personal identification number

pirating /'paɪrətɪŋ/ n U [26] illegally copying software programs

place value /'pleɪs ˌvæljuː/ n C [22] the value of an individual digit due to the position it occupies in a number, e.g. in the decimal system the second position from the right indicates tens and the third position from the right indicates hundreds

plotter /'plɒtə(r)/ n C [22] an output device used to output drawings onto paper

port /pɔːt/ n C [3] a connector at the back of a system unit of a PC that is used for connecting external devices to the CPU

portable (computer) /'pɔːtəbl/ n C [2] a computer that is small and light enough to be carried from place to place. It can usually be powered by batteries.

portable language /ˈpɔːtəbl ˌlæŋgwɪʤ/ n C [21] a language that can be easily converted for use on a number of different operating systems

post /pəʊst/ v [14] to display a message in a computer newsgroup or bulletin board

power supply /ˈpaʊə səˌplaɪ/ n C [3] the electrical component that provides filtered mains electricity at the correct voltage for a computer

printed circuit board /ˌprɪntɪd ˈsɜːkɪt ˌbɔːd/ n C [27] an electronic board that holds and connects the components of an electronic circuit

printer /ˈprɪntə(r)/ n C [2,7] a common output device used for printing the output of a computer on paper

procedure /prəˈsiːʤə(r)/ n C [19] a subsection of a high-level program designed to perform a particular function

process /ˈprəʊses/ v C [9] to manipulate the data according to the program instructions

processor /ˈprəʊsesə(r)/ n C [3,9] the part of a computer that processes the data

program /ˈprəʊɡræm/ n, v C [1,19, 20] a set of instructions written in a computer language that control the behaviour of a computer / to write a set of instructions for controlling a computer using a computer language

programmer /ˈprəʊɡræmə(r)/ n C [5,19, 20, 21] a person who writes computer programs

programming /ˈprəʊɡræmɪŋ/ n U [19, 20, 21] the processes of writing a computer program using a computer language

programming language /ˈprəʊɡræmɪŋ ˌlæŋgwɪʤ/ n C [14,19, 20, 21] a computer language used for coding computer programs

punched card /ˈpʌnʧt ˌkɑːd/ n C [25] an obsolete computer input medium consisting of a set of cards with holes punched in them

RAM /ræm/ n U [3] acronym for random access memory – memory that can be read and written to by the processor

random access /ˌrændəm ˈækses/ n U [8] a system of getting access to any location in a storage area in any order

read-only /ˌriːd ˈəʊnli/ adj [8] can only be read from and not written to

read-only memory /ˌriːd ˈəʊnli ˌmeməri/ n U [15] memory that contains programs and data that the user cannot change, for example, it may contain the programs required to start up a computer

read/write head /ˌriːd ˈraɪt ˌhed/ n C [8] the mechanism inside a disk or tape drive that is used for reading from and writing to the storage media

readout /ˈriːdaʊt/ n C [24] a display showing a measurement

record /ˈrekɔːd/ n C [17] a section of a database made up of related database fields

recycle bin /riːˈsaɪkl ˌbɪn/ n C [9] a program used to hide files that are no longer required and bring them back if they are required again. Emptying the recycle bin deletes the files completely.

refresh rate /rɪˈfreʃ ˌreɪt/ n C [7] the frequency at which the image is re-drawn on a display screen

register /ˈreʤɪstə(r)/ n C [22] a small unit of very fast memory that is used to store a single piece of data or instruction temporarily that is immediately required by the processor

resolution /ˌrezəˈluːʃn/ n C [7] a measure of the quality of a display screen in terms of the amount of graphical information that can be shown on the screen. This partly depends on the number of dots which make up the image.

ring topology /ˈrɪŋ təˌpɒləʤi/ n C [11] a physical layout of a network where all the computers are connected in a closed loop

robot /ˈrəʊbɒt/ n C [22] a mechanical device controlled by a computer

robotic /rəʊˈbɒtɪk/ adj [24] to do with robots

robotics /rəʊˈbɒtɪks/ n U [23] the study of robot systems

ROM /rɒm/ n U [22] acronym for read-only memory

router /ˈruːtə(r)/ n C [13] an electronic device that links different networks or parts of a network. It determines the path that a signal should take to reach its destination.

ruler /ˈruːlə(r)/ n C [16] a horizontal line containing markings indicating measurements on the display screen

run /rʌn/ v [8] to execute a program, i.e. to get a program to process the data

S

save /seɪv/ v [4,16] to copy a program or data to a storage device

scan /skæn/ v [1,6] to copy using a scanner

scanner /ˈskænə(r)/ n C [6] an optical input device that uses the reflection of light to copy text or graphics into a computer

screen (display) /skriːn/ n C [1, 4, 6] the front surface of a computer monitor where the output of a computer is displayed

script /skrɪpt/ n C [21] a small program written in a scripting language that is used to perform a simple function or to tie other programs together

scripting language /ˈskrɪptɪŋ ˌlæŋgwɪʤ/ n C [21] a simple computer language used for writing scripts that control computer applications

scroll /skrəʊl/ v [15] to move displayed information, either horizontally or vertically, on the screen

search engine /ˈsɜːʧ ˌenʤɪn/ n C [14] a program designed to find information on the World Wide Web according to data entered by the user. Search engines are usually accessed from special websites.

secondary storage /ˌsekəndri ˈstɔːrɪʤ/ n U [22] memory used for storing data that is not currently being used

serial mouse /ˈsɪəriəl ˌmaʊs/ n C [3] the type of mouse that is connected to the serial port at the back of the system unit of a PC

serial port /ˈsɪəriəl ˌpɔːt/ n C [3] the small connector at the back of the system unit of a PC that is used to connect a serial device such as a serial mouse or a modem. Two serial ports labelled COM1 and COM2 are usually provided on a PC.

server /ˈsɜːvə(r)/ n C [11] a main computer that provides a service on a network

SIMM /sɪm/ *n* C [2,15] acronym for single in-line memory module / a small electronic circuit board containing memory chips. SIMMs are designed to be plugged into memory slots.

smart card /'smɑːtkɑːd/ *n* C [23] a plastic card containing a processor and memory chip. It can be used to store large amounts of confidential data.

smart card reader /'smɑːtkɑːd ˌriːdə(r)/ *n* C [24] a device used for reading smart cards

smart clothes /'smɑːt ˌkləʊðz/ *n* Pl [24] clothes that contain embedded computing devices

software /'sɒftweə(r)/ *n* U [5] the programs and data used in a computer

solid state memory /ˌsɒlɪd ˌsteɪt 'meməri/ *n* U [6] electronic memory made from electronic chips

spacebar /'speɪsbɑː(r)/ *n* C [4, 21] the long key along the bottom of a keyboard used for inserting blank spaces in a document

speech recognition board /ˌspiːtʃ rekəg'nɪʃn ˌbɔːd/ *n* C [6] an electronic card that converts analogue sound signals into binary code to enable the computer to identify spoken words

spell(ing) checker /'spel ˌtʃekə(r)/ *n* C [20] a programmed function that checks the spelling of text in a document

spellcheck /'speltʃek/ *n, v* C [16] a check of spelling in a document / to check the spelling in a document

spreadsheet /'spredʃiːt/ *n* C [10,17] a type of application program with an array of cells that is used for calculating formulas

SQL /ˌeskjuː'el/ *n* U [28] abbreviation for structured query language, used for searching databases

stack /stæk/ *n* C [22] a temporary register that is used to store program instructions and data in a fixed sequence while the processor services an interrupt

star topology /'stɑː təˌpɒlədʒi/ *n* C [11] a physical layout of a network where all the computers are connected by separate cables to a central hub

status bar /'steɪtəs ˌbɑː(r)/ *n* C [16] a narrow band across the bottom of the screen that displays useful information for the user

storage device /'stɔːrɪdʒ dɪˌvaɪs/ *n* C [8] a piece of equipment used for reading from and writing to a storage medium

storage medium /'stɔːrɪdʒ ˌmiːdiəm/ *n* C [8] a material used for storing programs and data

sub-program /'sʌbprəʊgræm/ *n* C [27] a small program that performs a specific function and is part of a larger program

subfolder /'sʌbfəʊldə(r)/ *n* C [9] a way of subdividing a folder so that stored files can be organized into smaller groups

subnotebook (computer) /'sʌbnəʊtbʊk/ *n* C [2] a portable computer that is a little smaller than a notebook computer. It is small enough to fit inside a jacket pocket.

subscriber /səb'skraɪbə(r)/ *n* C [13] a user who becomes a member of a newsgroup

supercomputer /'suːpəkəmˌpjuːtə(r)/ *n* C [2] the most powerful type of mainframe computer

swipe card /'swaɪp ˌkɑːd/ *n* C [26] a plastic card with a magnetic strip running across it containing confidential data

synchronize /'sɪŋkrənaɪz/ *v* [22] to control the timing of events so that they take place in the correct order

syntax checker /'sɪntæks ˌtʃekə(r)/ *n* C [19] a computer function used when writing programs that checks for mistakes in the vocabulary or punctuation of the program

syntax error /'sɪntæks ˌerə(r)/ *n* C [19, 20] a mistake in a program due to a wrong word or punctuation symbol being used

system error /'sɪstəm ˌerə(r)/ *n* C [19] a program error caused by a fault affecting the operating system, usually due to a hardware failure

system unit /'sɪstəm ˌjuːnɪt/ *n* C [2, 9] the main part of a PC. It usually includes the electronics, power supply, hard disk drive, floppy disk drive, and a small loudspeaker. It may also include a CD-ROM drive and one or two other devices, but also has connectors to allow external devices to be attached.

systems analysis /ˌsɪstəms ə'næləsɪs/ *n* U [5, 27] the study of a system to determine how it can be computerized

systems program /ˌsɪstəms ˌprəʊgræm/ *n* C [27] a program that is part of a computer operating system and controls a basic function of a computer

systems programming /ˌsɪstəms ˌprəʊgræmɪŋ/ *n* U [21] the writing of systems programs

tab /tæb/ *n* C [9] a dialog box component that is used to switch between different sets of data

tab (2) /tæb/ *n, v* C [16] a fixed amount of space inserted into a line of text / to insert a fixed amount of space into a line of text

tag /tæg/ *n* C [21] a label used in HTML that is attached to a piece of text to mark the start or the end of a particular function

TCO-95 /ˌtiːsiːəʊ ˌnaɪnti 'faɪv/ *n* U [7] a standard of safety, health, and ergonomics produced by The Central Organization of Salaried Employees in Sweden

TCP/IP /ˌtiːsiːpiː: 'aɪ piː/ *n* U [27] abbreviation for transmission control protocol / Internet protocol / the official standard that determines the form of the signals used for transmitting data on the Internet.

terminal /'tɜːmɪnl/ *n* C [1, 28] a network device used to input and output data (usually a basic computer)

text box /'tekst ˌbɒks/ *n* C [9] a dialog box component that is used for entering text

title bar /'taɪtl ˌbɑː(r)/ *n* C [9] a narrow strip across the top of a window in a WIMP system that indicates what is inside the window

toner /'təʊnə(r)/ *n* U [10] the powder used inside laser printers

toolbar /'tuːlbɑː(r)/ *n* C [14] a row of icons displayed on a screen that start common program functions when clicked with a mouse

toolbox /'tuːlbɒks/ *n* C [18] a set of icons displayed on a screen for selecting common program editing functions. For example, a graphics package usually has a toolbox containing icons for choosing the line width, the line colour, for creating different common shapes, and for rotating images.

topology /tə'pɒlədʒi/ *n C* [11] the physical layout of a network

touchscreen /'tʌtʃ ˌskriːn/ *n C* [6, 24] an input device in the form of a monitor screen that responds when touched by the user

touchpad /'tʌtʃpæd/ *n C* [6] a cursor control input device that senses the movement of a finger across a flat surface

trackerball /'trækəbɔːl/ *n C* [6] a cursor control input device that has a ball on top that is moved by the user's fingers

translator program /træn'sleɪtə ˌprəʊgræm/ *n C* [19] a computer program that translates a program from one computer language to another

Trinitron /'trɪnɪtrɒn/ *adj* [7] the trade name for a type of monitor technology created by Sony

undo /ˌʌn'duː/ *v* [16] to restore a file to the condition it was in before the last change was made

unidirectional /ˌjuːnɪdaɪ'rekʃənl/ *adj* [22] designed to carry signals in or from one direction only

update /ˌʌp'deɪt/ *v* [15] to bring up to date, i.e. to change into the latest version

upgrade /ˌʌp'greɪd/ *v* [27, 28] to add components to improve the features or performance of a system

upgradeable /ʌp'greɪdəbl/ *adj* [3] designed so that components can be added to improve the features or performance of the system

USB /ˌjuː ˌes ˌbiː/ *n C* [3] abbreviation for universal serial bus. A standard way of connecting peripherals to a computer system.

VB /ˌviː'biː/ *n U* [28] abbreviation for Visual Basic / a general purpose programming language

VDU /ˌviːdiː'juː/ *n C* [27] abbreviation for visual display unit / another name for a computer monitor

video conference /ˈvɪdiəʊ ˌkɒnfərəns/ *n C* [12] a meeting between people that are a long distance apart, using cameras and display screens connected to a network to allow them to see and hear each other

video conferencing /ˌvɪdiəʊ'kɒnfərənsɪŋ/ *n U* [12] a form of communication over a network that uses video cameras so that the people taking part can see and hear each other

video memory /'vɪdiəʊ ˌmeməri/ *n U* [3] the memory used to store graphics data on a graphics card

videophone /'vɪdiəʊfəʊn/ *n C* [24] a telephone system that displays a video picture of the caller

video (VGA) port /'vɪdiəʊ ˌpɔːt/ *n C* [3] the small connector at the back of the system unit of a PC that is used to connect the monitor to the graphics card

virtual (reality) mouse /ˌvɜːtʃuəl 'maʊs/ *n C* [23] a cursor control input device used in VR systems

virtual reality /ˌvɜːtʃuəl ri'æləti/ *n U* [23] a simulated three dimensional environment that surrounds the user and is generated by a computer

virus /'vaɪrəs/ *n C* [10] a program written deliberately to damage data or cause a computer to behave in an unusual way

virus check /'vaɪrəs ˌtʃek/ *n, v C* [21] a test of a system to see if it contains a virus / to test a system to see if it contains a virus

voice mailbox /'vɔɪs ˌmeɪlbɒks/ *n C* [12] a storage area for spoken messages

voicemail /'vɔɪsmeɪl/ *n U* [12] a system of communication that uses computers to store spoken messages

VR /ˌviː 'ɑː(r)/ *n U* [23] abbreviation for virtual reality

VR glove /ˌviː ˌɑː 'glʌv/ *n C* [23] a virtual reality glove. See **dataglove**.

VR headset /ˌviː ˌɑː 'hedset/ *n C* [23] a virtual reality headset / an output device worn on the user's head in a virtual reality system. It displays three-dimensional graphics on a screen in front of the user's eyes

VR mouse /ˌviː ˌɑː 'maʊs/ *n C* [23] a virtual reality mouse

WAN /wæn/ *n C* [11] acronym for wide area network

Web, (the) /web/ *n U* [14] the common name for the World Wide Web

webpage /'webpeɪdʒ/ *n C* [6,14] a hyperlinked page in a web network system

website /'websaɪt/ *n C* [4,14] a set of pages on the World Wide Web

website address /'websaɪt əˌdres/ *n C* [4,14] the unique address that is used to access a website

White Pages, (the) /ˌwaɪt 'peɪdʒɪz/ *n Pl* [14] a website used for finding the email addresses of registered users

wide area network /ˌwaɪd ˌeəriə 'netwɜːk/ *n C* [11] computers connected together over a large distance

wildcard character /'waɪldkɑːd ˌkærɪktə(r)/ *n C* [17] a symbol used to represent any character or combination of characters

WIMP system /'wɪmp ˌsɪstəm/ *n C* [9] acronym for windows, icons, menus, and pointers / a common type of graphical user interface

window /'wɪndəʊ/ *n C* [9] a rectangular screen area containing a program, folder, or file in a WIMP system

Windows /'wɪndəʊz/ *n U* [9] the common name for Microsoft Windows, a popular graphical user interface developed by the Microsoft Corporation

word processing /ˌwɜːd'prəʊsesɪŋ/ *n U* [10,16] the process of typing and editing text using a word processor

word processor /ˌwɜːd'prəʊsesə(r)/ *n C* [10,16] a type of computer application program used for typing and editing text documents

workstation /'wɜːksteɪʃn/ *n C* [7] a desk area used for working with a computer system

World Wide Web, (the) /ˌwɜːld ˌwaɪd 'web/ *n U* [14] an information service on the Internet that allows document pages to be accessed using hyperlinks

Listening script

Unit 1 Everyday uses of computers

Task 4

Extract 1
We use a PC for writing letters, for playing games, to calculate our bills, and to connect with the Internet.
Extract 2
We've got electronic checkout tills with barcode readers. They read a special barcode on almost everything we sell. They calculate the bill for the customer. At the same time they send information to a larger computer, so we always know exactly what we've got in the store.
Extract 3
We make washing machines and refrigerators. The machines we use to make them are controlled by computers. We also use computers to calculate our wages, to keep the accounts, and to look after all materials and parts.
Extract 4
Our terminal links to airline offices. If you want to fly anywhere in the world, we can tell you at once if there's a seat on the flight you want. We can supply you with the tickets and we can reserve your hotel – all by computer.

Unit 2 Types of computer

Task 3

Part 1
A: I'm thinking of buying a computer, and I need some advice.
B: OK. What do you want to use it for?
A: For writing, maybe for games. I want it for the Internet.
B: For the Internet and games ... I recommend a multimedia computer.
A: What do you mean by a multimedia computer?
B: Well, it's more powerful than a basic computer. It's got sound and a CD-ROM or DVD drive. You can use it for high-quality graphics, animation, and video.
Part 2
A: What if I wanted ... I travel a lot, if I wanted something smaller, what's available?
B: There are portable computers. A multimedia notebook is probably best.
A: Is a notebook the smallest kind you can get?
B: No, you can get subnotebooks and even smaller handheld devices.

They're mostly used as organizers, as a diary, a 'to do' list, and that kind of thing. But for writing and general use a notebook is better.
A: OK, I think I'll go for a notebook. What other things do I need?
B: A printer ... and for the Internet, make sure you have a modem.
A: A modem?
B: Yes, it's a device for connecting your computer to a telephone line. You need it to connect to the Internet.

Unit 3 Parts of a computer

Task 3

A: What about things like power and speed, that sort of thing? What do I look for?
B: Well, power depends on speed and capacity – the speed of the processor and the capacity of the memory and the hard disk.
A: The speed of the processor?
B: How fast the computer processes data. Speed is usually given in megahertz or gigahertz. The faster the processor, the more powerful the computer.
A: And capacity?
B: How much storage space there is in the computer. Capacity depends on how much memory there is, how big the hard disk is. You measure RAM and video memory in megabytes. You've also got cache memory. That's in kilobytes. Always look for the highest numbers.
A: What about the hard disk?
B: Hard disk capacity is in gigabytes. Get a big hard disk for multimedia. Audio and video files use enormous amounts of space. Once again, the higher the numbers, the more powerful the computer.

Unit 4 Keyboard and mouse

Task 4

The keys on a computer keyboard can be arranged in many different ways. The most common way on a desktop PC is called the extended keyboard. The diagram shows an extended keyboard. The keys are in four main sections.
(pause)
The section known as the main keyboard has a key for each letter of the alphabet. It also has keys for the digits 0 to 9, punctuation marks like commas and full stops, and other common symbols.
(pause)
Above the main keyboard is a row of keys known as the function keys. This section includes the Escape key to the left and the Print Screen, Scroll Lock,

and Break keys to the right. The function keys labelled F1 to F12 don't have fixed functions. You can program them to perform different functions such as saving and printing.
(pause)
To the right of the main keyboard is a section known as the editing keys. This group includes keys which insert and delete data. It also includes the cursor keys, also called the arrow keys. These keys move the cursor around the screen.
(pause)
To the far right of the main keyboard is the numeric keypad. This section has keys for the digits 0 to 9 and for common mathematical symbols like plus and minus. The keys are arranged like the keys on an electronic calculator. You use these keys to input numerical data.

Unit 5 Interview: Student

Task 2

Part 1
INTERVIEWER: Tell me first of all about the course. What's the course called?
LYNSEY: Information Technology 3.
INTERVIEWER: How many students are there?
LYNSEY: In my class?
INTERVIEWER: Yes.
LYNSEY: Well, at the beginning seventeen.
INTERVIEWER: Right.
LYNSEY: But now there are fifteen.
INTERVIEWER: How many are men and how many women?
LYNSEY: Three girls and twelve boys.
INTERVIEWER: How long does the course last?
LYNSEY: A year.
INTERVIEWER: And it starts in August?
LYNSEY: September, and it goes on till June.

Tasks 5 and 6

Part 2
INTERVIEWER: Tell me about the timetable for your course.
LYNSEY: Well, on Monday I've got Communications 4. It lasts for two hours. Nine to eleven. Then it's Numeracy 3.
INTERVIEWER: Numeracy, that's some kind of maths?
LYNSEY: Yes, but it's more logic ... problem-solving.
INTERVIEWER: And do you have a break between classes?
LYNSEY: Yes, a half-hour break between eleven and eleven-thirty.
INTERVIEWER: Do you have other classes in the afternoon?
LYNSEY: Not on a Monday.
INTERVIEWER: What do you have on a Tuesday?

LYNSEY: Programming.
INTERVIEWER: Is that ... Well, tell me what it's about.
LYNSEY: We study computer languages like Pascal.
INTERVIEWER: So, Tuesday after the coffee break, what do you have?
LYNSEY: I'm sure it's Hardware ... No, it's Software, Computer Software.
INTERVIEWER: What happens in the Software class?
LYNSEY: You learn about operating systems and packages like databases.
INTERVIEWER: Do you have a class on a Tuesday afternoon?
LYNSEY: No, and nothing on a Wednesday.
INTERVIEWER: Nothing at all?
LYNSEY: No classes, but sometimes we visit companies. Tomorrow it's the Royal Bank ... to see how they use computers.
INTERVIEWER: What do you have on Thursday?
LYNSEY: Thursday, I'm not too sure. Hardware is last thing, half-past two.
INTERVIEWER: What happens in Hardware?
LYNSEY: You find out about all the different things inside a computer.
INTERVIEWER: What about Friday?
LYNSEY: We've got Networks first thing. We learn how computers work connected together.
INTERVIEWER: Anything on a Friday afternoon?
LYNSEY: That's IT in Business and Industry. It's applications. That's what our visit tomorrow is about. We have to write a report on each visit. Five or six pages long.

Task 7

Part 3
INTERVIEWER: You have a very busy time on this course but is there time for anything else? Is there a social side students can enjoy?
LYNSEY: There's football and there was a Students' Night in Betty's Bar for all the new students to get to know each other.
INTERVIEWER: Is there a Students' Union?
LYNSEY: Yeah, on the main campus. They organize discos, but I live out of town so I don't stay on at night, and I've got a job two nights a week.
INTERVIEWER: What do you do?
LYNSEY: I work in a hotel. I'm a waitress.
INTERVIEWER: So you work in a hotel part-time?
LYNSEY: Yes, just to make some extra money.
INTERVIEWER: Do you want to work in catering after you graduate?
LYNSEY: No, it's the worst hours for the worst pay.

Unit 6 Input devices

Task 4

Computers can listen to your voice and change what you say into a written message or into orders. Voice input is a great help to people who cannot use their hands. It also helps people like pilots who need their hands or eyes for other tasks.

There are five steps in voice input. Step 1: when you speak, you produce audio waves. A microphone changes these waves into electrical waves. That's Step 2. Inside the computer there's a speech recognition board. In Step 3, the speech recognition board processes the waves from the microphone to form a binary code for each word you say. A binary code is a pattern of zeroes and ones, for example, 01001100. Each word has its own code.

In Step 4, the computer compares the code with other codes in its memory to identify each word. When it finds the correct word, it displays it on the monitor screen. That's Step 5, the last step.

Unit 7 Output devices

Task 2

There are many different types of printer. These include inkjet, mono laser, and dye sublimation printers. Basically, you get what you pay for. The more you pay, the better the printer.
(pause)
Inkjet printers are the cheapest, but their print quality is not as good as the other two types of printer. They are expensive to run compared to mono laser printers, but are able to print in colour. Inkjets are the noisiest of the three types of printer.
(pause)
Mono laser printers are more expensive than inkjet printers but give you a better quality of black and white output. They cannot print in colour, but are the fastest type of printer and cost the least to run.
(pause)
Dye sublimation printers are the most expensive type of printer, but their print quality is extremely high. They are quiet in operation, but are relatively slow and very expensive to run.

Unit 8 Storage devices

Task 3

Part 1
The hard disk drive inside your PC is like a filing cabinet. Instead of paper, it stores everything electronically. It can hold all the software that runs on your system and all your personal files. It's a pretty important part of your computer.

A hard disk drive normally contains several disks. They're stacked on top of each other. There are five in the diagram. The drive motor spins the disks very quickly. It runs all the time your PC is in use.

There's a gap, a space, between each disk. We need the gaps so the read/write heads can move across the disks and reach all parts quickly. The head motor controls the read/write heads.

Task 5

Part 2
The space between the head and the disk surface is tiny. Even smoke from a cigarette can cause a crash. A crash is what happens when the head touches the surface of the disk. To keep out dust and smoke, the drive is inside a sealed case.

Unit 9 Graphical User Interface

Task 4

This is a picture of a computer screen with one window open. The window contains a dialog box. This one is the Find dialog box. You can see the name on the title bar at the top of the screen. You use this dialog box to find files or folders.
(pause)
Near the top of the window there are three tabs. The first tab is for searching by name and location. There are two other tabs: one for searching by date and the other for advanced searches.
(pause)
To search for a file by name and location, you type the name of the file in the drop-down list box called Named. In this example, the user wants to find all the document files. Then you choose the folder to search in using another drop-down list box labelled Look in. Here the user wants to look in the folder called Personal on the C drive. So the first drop-down list box is for the name, and the second drop-down list box is for the location.
(pause)
Between the Named and Look in drop-down boxes is a text box. In the text box you type any words which you want to look for. In this example, the user only wants documents with the word 'sport'.
(pause)
You start the search by clicking on the Find Now command button. Other buttons stop the search, start a new search, or browse the drives.

Unit 10 Interview: Computing Support Assistant

Task 2

Part 1: Introduction

INTERVIEWER: What do you like most about your job?

ANNE: I like, I like all aspects of the job. It's good to ..., it's varied so there's lots of interest.

INTERVIEWER: Are you ever bored?

ANNE: No, not really, because it's never the same things over and over again; it's different each time.

Problems

INTERVIEWER: What kind of problems are there? What kind of difficulties do people have?

ANNE: People have problems with the hardware, often with printers ... paper jamming. They also have problems finding options in the programs. Mostly with word processing.

INTERVIEWER: Are there any other hardware problems?

ANNE: Occasionally a computer freezes ... it hangs or freezes. It's usually a memory problem.

INTERVIEWER: Is it always the machine or is it sometimes the user?

ANNE: Sometimes it's the user. The printer isn't switched on, or there's no paper.

Task 3

Part 2: Keeping up to date

INTERVIEWER: How do you keep in touch with what's new in computing? It's changing all the time.

ANNE: Yeah, by the time you read something, it's out of date. Magazines are good for finding out what's new on the scene. The Internet also has information about new developments.

INTERVIEWER: Do you ever go on courses?

ANNE: Yes, they're a good way to keep up.

INTERVIEWER: What kind of courses?

ANNE: Well, operating systems change, so courses about the different functions on the operating system. And then there's the programs that people use, like the word processors and the spreadsheets and the databases. And the best way to understand them is by taking a course and trying them out yourself.

Unit 11 Networks

Task 7

Computers in a network can be connected in different ways, in different topologies. The three basic ways of connecting computers are: a star, a ring, and a bus topology.

(pause)

A star topology has a server computer at the centre and a separate cable connecting the server to each of the other computers in the network. The central server controls the flow of data in the network. If the central server fails, the whole network will fail.

(pause)

In a ring topology, each computer is connected to its neighbour in a circle. The data flows in one direction round the ring. If a cable breaks or one of the computers fails, the whole network will be affected.

(pause)

A bus topology has all the computers connected to a common cable. The data travels in both directions along the cable. If a computer fails, or we remove one from the network, it won't affect the other computers. Most networks are usually a combination of star, ring, and bus topologies to overcome some of these problems.

Unit 12 Communications

Task 4

ANSWERPHONE MESSAGE: Thank you for calling Taytron. The office is now closed, but if you'd like to leave a message after the tone, dial one for sales, dial two for maintenance, and dial three for all other enquiries.

JOHN BAILES: This is John Bailes with a message for Lenny Yang. I'm sorry to phone so late but I can't make our meeting at 10.15 tomorrow. There are no seats on the 8.30 flight. I've got a ticket for the 9.45 flight which lands at 10.30. If the traffic isn't too bad, I can be with you around 11.15, say 11.30 to be safe. So can we meet at half-past eleven tomorrow. If there's any problem, please email me tomorrow before 8.30. My address is "bailes, b-a-i-l-e-s@brandt.co.be". See you tomorrow.

Unit 13 The Internet 1: email and newsgroups

Task 4

Hi, I started my course last Monday. We've got classes every day from 8.45 until a quarter past four, apart from Fridays when we finish at 2.30. We can use the computer lab then, so I've taken the chance to send this message. The course is OK so far. 'Design and Make' is the best class. We've got to construct a project of our own. I'm thinking of a security alarm for my bike.

Staff are fine apart from Maths – no sense of humour – and I'm getting to know the rest of the class. There's an indoor sports centre we can use at lunchtimes, and a few of us have started kicking a ball about most days. We might get a team going.

Let me know how your course is going and how life is treating you. If you're free on the 17th, come over. I'm having a party at my flat. Nothing fancy, but you'll meet Sandra again.

Unit 14 The Internet 2: the World Wide Web

Task 6

1 This button stops your browser downloading information. Maybe because it's taking too long, or you're bored, or you've made a mistake in the address.

2 Whenever you find a page on the Web that you like and want to visit again, you can save it with this button.

3 This button will get you a fresh copy of any document you're looking at.

4 Click your mouse on this button and your browser will reload the last page you were at.

5 This button will take you back to the browser starting page.

Unit 15 Interview: Website Designer

Task 2

Part 1

INTERVIEWER: What kind of people want websites and why do they want websites?

SALADIN: People who feel they have to be on the Web because competitors are on the Web. They feel that not having a website is a sign of being behind the times.

INTERVIEWER: So other people have got a website and therefore they have to have one, too?

SALADIN: Yes. The better reason is people who have information they would normally provide free – like brochures, application forms, anything that would normally be sent out by mail.

INTERVIEWER: So it saves fax, postage ...

SALADIN: Printing costs. I think it's particularly useful for colleges and universities.

INTERVIEWER: Why is that?

SALADIN: Because they tend to have a large amount of information to distribute.

INTERVIEWER: If a client comes to you and asks you for a webpage, how do you set about designing a page for a client?

SALADIN: The first thing I would ask for is all their printed promotional material. I would look at all that material and then discuss with the client how much of it to put on the Web. The most important thing is to decide who is the audience for this website, who's it aimed at.

INTERVIEWER: Is there a danger of putting too much on?

SALADIN: There's certainly a danger of putting too much on. Also, the client has to make a clear decision about how much time or money they're going to spend to keep the pages updated.

INTERVIEWER: Aha, so it's not enough simply to have a page, you need regular maintenance of that page.

SALADIN: Right, so these are the first two questions – who is it aimed at and how often will it be updated?

Task 3

Part 2

SALADIN: Once we've decided what materials should be put on, there are a couple of basic principles to follow. One is that there should never be any dead ends, you should never reach a page which has no ...

INTERVIEWER: Ah, which doesn't go anywhere?

SALADIN: ... Which has no links to take you back to somewhere else. So that's one principle. And the other principle is to try to limit the number of steps that have to be taken from the main home page to any other page. I would normally aim for a maximum of four steps.

INTERVIEWER: Do people give up if there are more than two or three links, they simply give up, is that a problem?

SALADIN: Some people will give up. Others will just never find the information, there are too many diversions. Another principle is not to have too many links to scroll through on one page. If you have a page which has 150 links and you have to keep scrolling through them, people will give up ... they'll never find the links at the bottom.

INTERVIEWER: What about graphics, sound and animations, and all these multimedia features? What's your feeling about these?

SALADIN: Always ask why is it there? That's the first thing. And if it's there simply because it makes the page look nicer, think quite carefully about whether to put it there or not. The more of that sort of thing you have, the more time it will take to download the pages. Another factor to bear in mind is that there are still a lot of users with less sophisticated browsers than Netscape or Microsoft Explorer, and if you make the use of the page dependent on graphics and so on, you'll exclude these users.

INTERVIEWER: So no dead-ends, no more than four steps from home, and pictures have to serve a serious purpose.

Task 4

Part 3

SALADIN: Another aspect of designing pages is to break the information into relatively small sections.

INTERVIEWER: Is that just because of the size of the screen, what you can see at one time?

SALADIN: It's partly that, but it's also to do with download time and printing. People can find they're printing forty pages of a document, most of which they don't want.

INTERVIEWER: Is it a big temptation to add links to similar organizations? Is there strength in that, or is there a danger in that?

SALADIN: In most cases it's a big strength. Browsers who come across your page, if they discover that your page is a very good gateway to all sorts of interesting sites, will bookmark your page because they know it's a good way to get to all the other sites. If they're coming back to it, they're exposed to your message every time. One final point: it is useful to have on the front page something brief which catches the reader, which says 'this is who we are'.

Unit 16 Word processing

Task 3

The diagram shows a Microsoft Word screen display. The title bar at the top of the screen shows the program you're using and the name of the file, in this case Printer.

Below the title bar is the menu bar. The nine items on this bar each give access to a pull-down menu – File, Edit, View, and so on.

The standard toolbar is next. It contains buttons for the most commonly used commands such as Open documents, Print, and Spellcheck. Each button contains an icon.

The formatting toolbar is below the standard toolbar. You use it to alter the font – that's the typeface – and the style of letters – bold, italic, or underlined – and generally to alter the appearance of your document.

The bar at the bottom of the screen shows more information about the document you're working on. For example, it shows which page you're on. It's called the status bar. In this example, the user is on page 1.

Unit 17 Databases and spreadsheets

Task 8

1 Cell D two *(pause)* equals B two plus C two.

2 Cell A seven *(pause)* Saturday.

3 Cell B five *(pause)* one thousand and four.

4 Cell C seven *(pause)* six hundred and fourteen.

5 Cell B nine *(pause)* equals sum B two to B eight.

6 Cell E two *(pause)* equals D two times seventeen point five per cent.

Unit 18 Graphics and multimedia

Task 3

Extract 1

MARK: Right. It's a very simple graphic. It's a square for the wall, a triangle for the roof, two small squares for windows, and a rectangle for the door.

(pause)

MARK: Right, we'll start with a box shape, a square. Point with the cursor at the image you want in the toolbox. That's the rectangle. Click with your left mouse button. Now move the pointer to the screen.

ERIC: So the cursor turns into that sort of gun-sight thing.

MARK: Yeah. Press and hold down Shift. Now drag the pointer to make the square the size you want. Keep your finger on the left button. Then let go.

Extract 2

MARK: Now you want another square for a window. Just the same way. Point with your cursor, click with the left button, and hold Shift down.

Extract 3

MARK: Say you want the next square to be exactly the same as that one, right? Click on the Select box and then drag your cursor over the first window. Make sure it's all included. Now go into the Edit menu. Click on Copy; then on Paste. See how the second window appears? Now click on it and drag it into the house. You can get rid of the dotted lines by clicking outside them.

Extract 4

MARK: Now you want a door. So you go back to the rectangle. Click with your left mouse button, drag the rectangle to the size you want and release the button.

ERIC: You don't need Shift?

MARK: No, that's for squares, not rectangles.

Extract 5

ERIC: We want a triangle next.

MARK: Click on Polygon. That gives you any angled shape. Start at one corner of the house and draw one side of the roof. Then click on the opposite corner and the lines join up by themselves.

Extract 6

ERIC: It's a bit steep.

MARK: OK, we can rub it out easily. Click on Eraser. You see, your cursor becomes a little square. You can erase the first roof and make a lower one.

Unit 19 Programming

Task 3

Part 1

The circle is a CONNECTOR symbol. It appears when two separate paths through a process come together. It's always empty. You don't find any text, numbers, or symbols in it. Just the circle.

The parallelogram is the INPUT or OUTPUT symbol. It looks like a rectangle with two sloping sides. We use it when data has to be input or output. It contains words like *Input* or *Print*.

The ellipse is the START or STOP symbol. It looks like a rounded rectangle. It's used at the beginning and end of a flowchart, so it will contain the word *Start* or the word *Stop*.

The diamond shape is the DECISION symbol. It's used whenever a decision has to be made. Often it contains comparison functions such as less than or greater than. It has a *Yes* or *True* branch at one corner and a *No* or *False* branch at another.

The ordinary rectangle is the OPERATION or PROCESS symbol. It indicates the kind of operation. It will contain words like *add*, *subtract*, *multiply*, *divide* or *make equal to*.

Task 5

Part 2

This is a flowchart for calculating a tax, called sales tax, which is charged when you buy certain things. The flowchart begins with a Start symbol. Then you input the initial cost of the item. We'll call the initial cost C.

Next there's a decision. There are two rates of tax, 15% and 10%. The program must decide which rate to use. We'll call the rate R.

R depends on the initial cost. If the cost is greater than 100, the program follows the Yes route and sets the tax at 15%. Otherwise, the program follows the No route and sets the tax at 10%.

The two different paths, or routes, come together again at the connector symbol and continue along the same route. Then there's an operation. Sales tax is calculated by multiplying the cost, C, by the rate, R. Finally the amount of tax is printed out and the program stops.

Unit 20 Interview: Analyst/Programmer

Task 2

Part 1

INTERVIEWER: Who's it for?

COLIN: Basically for young adults with number problems.

INTERVIEWER: Oh, I like that, that's good.

COLIN: *(reading from the screen)* The fire is 5.4 kilometres away. The fire engine has gone this far. How far is the fire now?

INTERVIEWER: There's a calculator.

COLIN: Yes, you use the calculator to type in your answer.

INTERVIEWER: It doesn't do the calculation for you?

COLIN: No ...

INTERVIEWER: ... but it makes it a bit more interesting.

COLIN: Yes. And if you get it wrong ... the building burns down. (Oh no!) But, if you get it right, there's an animation of the fire engine putting the fire out. (Oh, I see.) The fire engine moves along and a spout of water appears on the screen. The next picture is the building without a mark on it. (Gosh.)

Task 3

Part 2

COLIN: We found with some people that there was a lot of stigma about learning how to count again.

INTERVIEWER: Almost as bad as not being able to read?

COLIN: Yes, the problem for them was being in a classroom with a teacher. So we designed a program they could use themselves at their own speed.

INTERVIEWER: How do they use it?

COLIN: In a computing lab. The machines are networked. One contains the data store and an administrative package for the teacher.

INTERVIEWER: What's in the administrative package?

COLIN: It allows the teacher to create groups and add students to groups, and it also has stats on their performance. (Oh, right.) Every time a student accesses a module, it records how much they've done, how long they've been at it, and how many times they've called Help.

INTERVIEWER: How did you test it? This is an important part of programming, isn't it?

COLIN: Oh, yes. We test the code in-house. You can't debug your own code – you need someone else to look at it. So you give it to a colleague and they try to break it. After that we test the program in schools – three schools with three or four machines as a pilot test.

INTERVIEWER: What sort of problems come up?

COLIN: Well, with Dante the graphics caused a lot of problems. Because we were working with state of the art machines, we forgot that schools don't have the same technology. Our graphics looked horrible on a lower-grade machine. We had to rescan and start programming for the simplest machine.

INTERVIEWER: What about syntax errors?

COLIN: Syntax errors are typos, generally. If you type PRINT and you hit I too many times, you get PRIIIINT. The compiler will catch that. That's the first kind of error, compilation errors. The second type are linking errors.

INTERVIEWER: Linking errors?

COLIN: A linking error is when you refer to something that isn't there. For example, a line of code in a library. When you use the same function over and over again, you don't write it each time. You refer to a library on the drive. Then you're down to the third type, logic errors. They happen when you're not awake, when you're not thinking properly. For example, you can make the program repeat a section of code until a condition is reached. And if you never reach that condition, it will run and run and run for ever.

Task 4

Part 3

INTERVIEWER: Is programming quite stressful?

COLIN: Very. But I'm often asked to fix something on the network. So that gives me a break. We never spend a whole day, 9 to 5, programming. It's impossible.

INTERVIEWER: Do you work on paper at all?

COLIN: Yes, at the design stage it's better to get as far away from computers as you can. We've got a canteen and we go through to the canteen with a pad of paper and cup of coffee and work it out.

INTERVIEWER: You say 'we'. Do you work as part of a team?

COLIN: Yes, there's myself and three developers, and two who work on graphics. Dante would have been impossible for one person to write. It took us six months to develop it properly. It was quite a good project because it was easy to divide up the work. There were the modules to do, the database design, and the database access. There was the client interface and the student interface so people were assigned to different sections.

INTERVIEWER: How many computer languages do you normally work in?

COLIN: Normally? C plus plus, we're using Active Server pages which involves HTML and JavaScript. You can use VB, Visual Basic, but if you use Visual Basic you're tying yourself to Microsoft and we want anybody to be able to run our programs. And Dante was written in Delphi.

INTERVIEWER: How do you keep up? Things are changing amazingly quickly.

COLIN: Well, I subscribe to two magazines, PCPro and Byte. I also pick up Dr Dobb's Journal when I can. Oh, and at work we subscribe to Microsoft Developer. We get two CDs from them four times a year. It's basically an electronic library with manuals, articles, and everything you need.

INTERVIEWER: This must take up your free time as well as work time.

COLIN: Yeah, it does, but I enjoy it, especially at the end of the day when things are beginning to go well. I hate it when you've got to go home, because you might lose it the next day.

Unit 21 Languages

Task 4

line ten, rem averages
line twenty, CLS
line thirty, print, open quotes, type nine nine nine to indicate end of data, close quotes
line forty, print
line fifty, sum equals zero
line sixty, counter equals zero
line seventy, print, open quotes, please enter a number, close quotes
line eighty, input number
line ninety, do while number is not equal to nine nine nine
line one hundred, sum equals sum plus number
line one hundred and ten, counter equals counter plus one
line one hundred and twenty, print, open quotes, please enter the next number, close quotes
line one hundred and thirty, input number
line one hundred and forty, loop
line one hundred and fifty, average equals sum divided by counter
line one hundred and sixty, print, open quotes, the average of the numbers is colon, space, close quotes, semi-colon, average
line one hundred and seventy, end

Unit 22 Low-level systems

Tasks 4 and 5

Part 1

The Central Processing Unit, the CPU, has three main parts: the Control Unit, the Arithmetic and Logic Unit, and Registers. These components are connected to the rest of the computer by buses.

The Arithmetic and Logic Unit, ALU for short, performs arithmetic functions such as ADD and SUBTRACT, and logic operations such as AND, OR, and NOT. The Control Unit makes the computer carry out each instruction of a program in the right order and controls the operation of all hardware, including input and output devices and the other parts of the CPU.

Registers are temporary storage areas for instructions or data. They work under the direction of the control unit. They hold the instructions or data *immediately* required for an operation, whereas main memory stores data required *in the near future*. Registers work at high speed.

Tasks 6 and 7

Part 2

A bus is a group of parallel wires which carry electrical signals between different parts of the computer. Some buses are bidirectional. They allow data to flow in either direction. Most computers have three main buses: the data bus, the address bus, and the control bus.

The data bus is a bidirectional bus. It carries data and instructions from the memory to the CPU and from the CPU to memory.

The address bus is a unidirectional bus. Data flows one way only. It carries addresses from the processor to memory. The addresses identify places in the memory where data or instructions may be found or stored.

The control bus is bidirectional. It carries instructions to and from the CPU and other parts of the computer. It's a collection of lines which carry different signals. For example, the clock line carries a signal from the clock chip to synchronize the operations of the processor.

Unit 23 Future trends 1

Task 2

Part 1

Virtual reality (VR) means using 3-D graphics to create an imaginary world, or virtual world, which surrounds the user.

You need special equipment to use VR. A VR headset or head-mounted display shows graphics on a screen in front of your eyes. As you turn your head, the picture on the screen moves around too, so it feels as if you are in a 3-D world. A dataglove, or VR glove, is a glove with pressure pads which make your hand feel as if it's picking up objects or touching surfaces. You use a kind of mouse called a VR mouse, 3-D mouse, or virtual mouse to move around in virtual space.

Task 3

Part 2

Virtual reality is already being used in many ways – in medicine, entertainment, and design. But VR is not yet very realistic. As techniques improve, though, VR could seem so real that you could live a virtual life – having many of your experiences through VR. For example, virtual travel systems could take you on a virtual holiday, letting you experience other parts of the world through a VR headset.

Some people even think that VR headsets might be replaced by DNI – Direct Neural Interface – that would stimulate your brain cells to give you a virtual experience. A brain implant would work in a similar way, but would give you special skills, like being able to speak a new language or play an instrument, without having to learn it.

Unit 24 Future trends 2

Task 4

Part 1

In the near future all schools and libraries will be linked together to form a National Grid for Learning – just like the electricity grid which connects all consumers. Each pupil will have a palmtop linked to the school network and to the Internet. All pupils from the age of nine will have email accounts. All communications between the Department for Education and schools will be by computer links. Learning and administration will be paper-free.

The advantages are obvious. Pupils will have access to a world of learning. The resources available through the Grid will be far greater than any one school can provide.

In addition, all pupils will become familiar with information technology at an early stage in their school life. Their computer skills will help them when they leave school and enter college or go into work. All study and most jobs in the future will require computer literacy. These developments will equip our pupils for an IT-based future.

Email will allow pupils to communicate easily with other pupils in different parts of the country and in different parts of the world. It will develop communication skills and encourage an international outlook.

Finally, by freeing teachers from paperwork, IT will give teachers more time for their real job of inspiring students.

Task 5

Part 2

There are real dangers in making school education so dependent on computers.

Easy access to online resources will not help pupils to develop original ideas. Instead, they will simply copy and paste text from online encyclopaedias or even download complete essays.

More time communicating with machines means less time to communicate with real people. We will produce students who are not good at communicating their ideas to others and working as part of a team.

Another danger is that the National Grid might lead to centralization. What I mean is that all schools will have access to the same centrally produced content and will do the same things. We need to encourage schools to develop their own ideas.

Experience in the US has shown that greater use of computers has failed to raise educational standards in schools. Instead of buying computers, it's far better to spend the money on teaching reading and numeracy, and on 'hands-on' field trips.

Unit 25 Interview: IT Manager

Tasks 3 and 4

Part 1 Past developments

TOM: I started in computing in 1965 on an ICT 1904 which was a transistorized machine. Prior to that we shared with another company an old valve machine. The 1904 was a multi-programming machine with no disks and 16k of memory.

INTERVIEWER: 16k! Was it punched card input?

TOM: Paper tape input and output. Magnetic tape drives ... which we had a lot of trouble with. So I was lucky enough to get into the early stages of computing and see the developments from there.

INTERVIEWER: When did things really begin to lift off here? When did you see the most rapid growth?

TOM: Eh, oh dear, well, that started from 1974 when microprocessors

came in. Then 1980 brought a big step forward in computing power with the first PCs, and it's just mushroomed since then. Through the eighties there were enormous changes in hardware as more efficient, faster, smaller machines came in. There were staggering changes just in the electrical load. We were dropping by around a megawatt a year in consumption if you took into account the air-conditioning as well as the machine.

INTERVIEWER: Of course, they had to be in air-conditioned rooms.

TOM: As the computers became more powerful, we used less and less power.

INTERVIEWER: And did the number of staff involved grow?

TOM: No, it dropped. At the peak we had about, there were about forty of us, but machines got more reliable.

INTERVIEWER: Were they very unreliable at first?

TOM: Oh yes, the early days were difficult because the hardware was unreliable. Four hours between crashes. Constant battles with the suppliers. It wasn't until 1980 that we got really reliable machines. Now, of course, we have things like Crays.

INTERVIEWER: When did you get the first Cray?

TOM: Oh, it must have been in the early nineties, I suppose.

INTERVIEWER: What's the most significant date for you?

TOM: 1990 I see as a significant date. 1990 was the change from central computing to distributed computing. PCs on desks rather than central mainframes.

Task 5

Part 2 Future developments

INTERVIEWER: What do you think is going to happen in the next few years? What do you think will be the big developments in computing?

TOM: I think speech recognition could be big. I think people who don't have very good keyboard skills will want to look at speech recognition. We're going to live in the Web browser environment a lot more.

INTERVIEWER: Does that mean shared software of all kinds?

TOM: Yes, I think it means that you'll ... you'll access multiple applications through a common interface, based on the sort of Web technology. On the other hand, so much effort is being put into what we're doing now that change is going to be difficult. People are not going to want to change unless there's some good reason for doing so. We're really achieving what most people want to do at the moment. People can send email, they can do their word processing, and

things like that. A lot of the new releases are based on just commercial pressure. The companies have to keep on ..., like motor cars, they have to have the latest model. Often there's no significant change. In general, things will get cheaper and faster which will improve performance and make software more efficient.

INTERVIEWER: What about video conferencing and that sort of thing?

TOM: Well, we have it already. It's OK, if it saves you a journey overseas it's maybe all right, but if it saves you going across town you wouldn't bother. You'd rather go out and see somebody face to face.

INTERVIEWER: Teaching, are there any developments there?

TOM: Computer teaching is still difficult, I think. It's good for reinforcing, it's good for practising, it's good for working on your own. But I don't see computers replacing good teaching. That's still going to be required. Computer teaching may be used more but I don't see it replacing courses.

Unit 26 Issues in computing

Task 3

How can you protect your computer from unauthorized access? Various ways have been developed to ensure that only the right people can access a system. We can divide these methods into three groups: what you have, what you know, and who you are.

What you have
You may have a plastic card, a swipe card, to get into rooms where there are computers. In some companies, workers wear an active badge, an ID card with an embedded chip, which signals where the wearer is at any time. The company knows immediately if an employee enters a computer room.

What you know
Computers are often protected by passwords. You have to know the correct password to enter the system, in the same way that you have to know your personal identification number to get money out of a bank cash machine.

Who you are
Every individual is unique. Some security systems use individual body characteristics. For example, your computer can be protected by a fingerprint recognition system. The computer will only respond when it reads your unique fingerprint. A new product called *Facelt* uses face recognition to protect individual files. It will only give access to a file if your face matches stored pictures of

authorized users. However, beards and spectacles can cause problems. Voice recognition and identification by the retina of the eye are other means to protect access.

Some systems use a combination of these groups. For example, an ID card *and* a password.

Unit 27 Careers in computing

Task 5

1

Before I write a program, I have to carry out a feasibility study in the company. The aim is to see whether a new program would be better than the methods they use at present. I have to observe what the users do, speak to them, and make an analysis of their systems. It's very important to speak to the actual users, not just the managers.

2

My job is to persuade customers that it's worth investing in new computer systems or extending the systems they already have. But it's not enough simply to sell the systems. We have to keep in touch after the sale and make sure things are working well, and to provide any backup the client needs. That's the only way to build up trust with a customer and to get new orders. It's a very competitive market.

3

I'm called out if there's a fault on the network. We try to solve the problem by phone at first, but if that doesn't work, we have to go and look for ourselves. It could be anything: the software, the server, even the cabling. Sometimes the problem is the user! You have to be good at working out where the problem is.

4

It's my job to try out new components before they're used in our computers. It's not only how well the components work that matters, they also have to meet health and safety requirements. I need to write reports and make recommendations on my findings. If problems arise after the components have been installed, I'm the person who has to find the solution.

5

I have to change the specifications for a system into a logical sequence that can be programmed. The language I choose for coding will depend on various factors such as what type of program it is, and where it's going to be used. A lot of testing has to be done and I use the feedback to decide where improvements can be made.

Unit 28 Interview: Systems Manager

Tasks 2 and 3

Part 1

INTERVIEWER: What sort of company do you work for?

BILL: I work for the largest brewer in the UK.

INTERVIEWER: And how long have you worked for them?

BILL: I've been there for almost twenty-five years.

INTERVIEWER: And what's your post there? What's your job title?

BILL: I'm a Systems Manager.

INTERVIEWER: And what are your duties?

BILL: Basically, I look after the systems for the Technical Services division. Technical Services make sure that the beer gets into the glass in good condition.

INTERVIEWER: OK, so what are your specific duties?

BILL: I'm responsible for existing systems and their running, maintenance, and general order. I'm responsible for the systems infrastructure we use – networks, PCs, and other devices – and I'm responsible for new systems development.

INTERVIEWER: Can you give me an example of a system?

BILL: Yes, here's an example of an operational system. We have 2,600 pubs and 350 service engineers. If the beer dispenser stops working in a pub, that's a serious matter for the publican. He or she rings in with the fault. That's logged on the system. We telephone an engineer who goes to the pub, investigates the fault and fixes it, and records details of what he's done on a handheld device he carries with him. The details of all the work he's done that day are downloaded to a PC at the end of the day, and then sent up in the middle of the night to our mainframe system and processed there. The activity is recorded, and the parts used, and how long it took. Our stock database is adjusted, and new parts ordered to make up stock where necessary. Everything is handled by one system.

INTERVIEWER: You're also responsible for developing new systems.

BILL: Nowadays we tend to buy packages or have packages modified to our requirements.

INTERVIEWER: Why do you buy in systems and not produce them in-house?

BILL: It's now standard procedure to buy in. When I started, we would always write our own. But there's so much available now and people expect a high standard of sophistication from a system.

In-house development would take too long and be enormously expensive.

INTERVIEWER: How do you choose a system?

BILL: If you're looking for a system, you see what the market has to offer and you make up a shortlist. You get the shortlisted companies in to make presentations. In addition to a system that meets your needs, you're looking for a company which is financially sound and has a good track-record, and can take you to sites with satisfied customers. You're looking really for a business partner. It's a long-term relationship. The fact that you spend fifty to sixty thousand pounds on the software is almost immaterial compared with the investments you're going to put into your own company, in getting the system commissioned and configured, and working and documented, and everything else.

Part 2

INTERVIEWER: How many systems do you have running?

BILL: In the whole Beer Division there are many hundreds of systems.

INTERVIEWER: It must be enormously complicated, because you'll have programs of all sorts of ages.

BILL: Yes, we have some systems twenty years old. One problem I have is to ensure that old and new systems can interface.

INTERVIEWER: How do you protect your systems?

BILL: Everything is on the mainframe and it's all backed up. It's all protected. You can't just go along and change something. It's a protected environment. There are passwords. You need several signatures to change anything. The databases are backed up on cartridges and taken off site to a fireproof store. There are contingency plans and disaster plans so that even if there was a nuclear strike we could be back in business in a couple of weeks.

INTERVIEWER: What about the future? Do developments on the hardware side make any difference to your systems?

BILL: Well, you can hold more information online than you could before. You can have much more history, bigger files, but what is making much more difference to our company is faster communications. We have our own internal email system and there are links from there into the Internet.

INTERVIEWER: So the future for you is faster information flow.

BILL: Yes – which means you don't need to have so many bits of paper.

INTERVIEWER: So a paper-free office?

BILL: There's no such thing and there never will be.